A CRITIC AT LARGE

BY THE SAME AUTHOR

Celtic Dawn
Sport is My lifeline
Oliver St John Gogarty
Brendan Behan
A Terrible Beauty is Born
Travels with Ulick

*

POEMS AND PLAYS

Life Styles
Sputnik
Three Noh Plays

*

Irish Tales and Sagas

A Critic at Large

ULICK O'CONNOR

THE MERCIER PRESS
DUBLIN and CORK

The Mercier Press Limited
4 Bridge Street, Cork
24 Lower Abbey Street, Dublin 1

O'Connor, Ulick
A critic at large.
1. English literature — 20th century —
History and criticism
I. Title
820.9'00912 PR471

ISBN 0-85342-730-5

Printed by Litho Press Co. Ltd., Midleton, Co. Cork

Contents

Preface

These items appeared in *The Sunday Independent* to which I contribute a weekly column. They have been selected from a large number of contributions and, I hope, form a coherent whole.

Writing about books can be the devil. One has to read the volumes – carefully, if justice is to be done to the author. Fortunately, I am a readaholic so that part of the business is not unpleasant. To get a piece into shape that will convey the flavour and atmosphere of the work is another matter. Drawers of rewritten pages will attest to this fact. Despite the labour, the result must read easily on the eye. If I have achieved this, the first rule of the essayist, I shall be content.

1. Lennox Robinson

It is a pain in the neck to have known a man and not realise you have been associated with a genius until after his death. I knew Lennox Robinson when I was in my twenties and he was the most delightful company you could find, as well as being extremely kind to a young man like myself trying to push his pen. But I had no idea Lennox was the writer he was. I couldn't really have known because they never did his plays in the Abbey at that time. He was on the Board but also on the hard stuff and he simply was too much of a gentleman to fight his corner as he should have. When the Abbey presented *The White-headed Boy* three years ago I got my first glimpse into Lennox, the playwright. Then the overwhelming success of *Drama at Inish,* fifty years after it was first produced, made it clear that Lennox didn't write for an age, but for all time. What a perfect play. Ibsen might have written it if he'd had an Irish sense of humour. But since he hadn't, one can only surmise that, had the old Norwegian seen it, he would have nodded his head in approval having laughed his way through the evening's entertainment. Is there any better example of what the realist dramatists tried to do than the simple words Lennox puts into the mouth of Annie, the hotel owner's wife in *Drama at Inish*. 'Did you ever see a big stone in a field? You might be sitting by it, idle like, some sunny afternoon, and then for no reason at all you turn it over. And what would you see. Worms. Little beetles that run this way and that. Horrible little creepies that'd make your stomach turn and you put the stone back as quick as you could or you'd run away.'

Now Colin Smythe has brought out a selection of

Lennox Robinson's plays, chosen and with an introduction by Dr Christopher Murray. Lovers of literature are very lucky in their Dublin academics these days. They are producing books for us about writers who are not fashionable but who should be because of the importance of their work. Dr Augustine Martin has helped to popularise James Stephens and now Dr Murray is doing the same thing for Lennox Robinson: this is the proper relationship, of course, which should exist between the literary public and the academic community but it is not always so.

Dr Murray has chosen six of Robinson's plays to show not only his technical ability as a playwright but 'his love of Ireland and its people'. Lennox was the son of a Cork rector and spent much of his life amongst the Anglo-Irish but he was a convinced Sinn Féiner and believed that England had no business to try to run the affairs of this country. In one of the plays Dr Murray has selected, *Patriots,* a Fenian comes out of prison in 1912 to find the country pacified with political promises and temporary prosperity. When he's told his views are out of date, James Nugent (whose character is surely based on Tom Clarke) replies: 'Out of date. They were supposed to be out of date then. Mitchel was out of date, Emmet was out of date, but I tell you that until Ireland gets out of date from North 'til South she'll never win anything.'

To those, who after the Rising called it futile, Lennox himself replied that they had 'joined the ranks of the hunkerers'. A few weeks after Easter 1916 he was at a Boucicault play in the Queen's when 'The Wearing of the Green' was sung and the whole audience joined in. 'The old feeling of the unreality of the words vanished and I saw – as I believe everyone in the hall saw – the long grave at Arbour Hill, Roger Casement lying between the malefactors and – Hush! Let there be silence – or tears.'

The splendid thing about Lennox is that he did not

dismiss the class he came from. He had worked in close association with too many people of ascendancy background, Horace Plunkett, Dermod O'Brien and Lord Mounteagle, not to know that they were dedicated Irishmen even if their politics were different from his. Lennox's play, *The Big House,* catches the fine qualities of many of the Anglo-Irish landowners and the dreadful dilemma in which they found themselves in 1922 when England had deserted them, having used methods of warfare that none of these Irishmen could have condoned.

In the character of St Leger Alcock, the owner of Ballydonal House, Lennox Robinson has caught the complex nature of the Anglo-Irish character. Alcock's daughter, Kate, says when she is asked to marry an English officer: 'It's my life here. I don't like marrying out of my life, out of my class. I don't mean that in a snobbish way. I'm sure the Despards are as good as we are – but they are different. They are English.'

Where Lennox scores as a true artist in this play is that he doesn't make the English wife of St Leger Alcock unlikeable. She is, in fact, the most reasonable person in the play. But, somehow, she's 'different'.

It is interesting to learn from Dr Murray's introduction that Lennox Robinson wrote twenty-five plays. This is an impressive output. He also wrote a light but illuminating biography of Dermod O'Brien as well as a memoir of Major Brian Cooper which is not included here in the select check list compiled by Frances J. French. As an actor Lennox had a considerable success when he played Henry IV in Pirandello's version for the Dublin Drama League in the twenties. In the 1950s he wrote a column in the *Irish Press* which was widely read and which was an indication of his ability to touch the popular pulse.

I remember the last time I saw dear Lennox was among the sweet-pea which he grew in his beloved Sheridan House for actors in Mount Street. He swayed among the flowers as gentle and pliable as they, and his voice, seemed to come and go with the wind.

He had a damned good Protestant funeral in a packed St Patrick's Cathedral. His coffin stood just to the left of where that other Irish patriot writer, Jonathan Swift, is buried in the aisle of the cathedral. I had felt uneasy as I walked into the service. Outside the cathedral stood numbers of gentlemen in morning coats, including a former Taoiseach, but they were making no effort to enter the church. The Archbishop of Dublin had forbidden attendance at Protestant services. I felt that religion did not demand this discourtesy and passed the picket. That's how it was in Dublin then.

Lennox, I'm sure, would be glad to know that it's somewhat different today.

17 April 1983

2. Sitwelliana

Sir Osbert and Edith Sitwell, brother and sister, hugged the limelight in England as far as the writing profession was concerned between the wars. They knew exactly how to get into the scandal columns of the English dailies and manipulated the media with as much skill as Brendan Behan later did. Edith, with her bangles clanking and aquamarine ring sending out warning signals, was always good for a news item in next day's columns. 'Please have Anthony Hartley stuffed and put in a glass case with moth balls,' she wrote to *The Spectator* after an adverse criticisim had appeared and added that the staff were 'too busy playing yo-yo with their Adam's apples at belated Browning Societies' to be in a position to appreciate her poetry.

She accused the poet Geoffrey Grigson of being unable to write anything except 'examine the sex life of a winkle', and when asked to read her poems on a platform with Ann Ridler and Roy Fuller, replied that 'it was like asking Sarah Bernhardt to discuss the art of acting with two nice young people who had appeared twice in some remote and sparsely peopled and dusty provincial theatre.'

Osbert took his sister's side in these rows and was furious once when he forgot to snub Noel Coward (who had insulted Edith) at a reception in Buckingham Palace: 'The brute apologised to me the other day and I forgot to kick him down the stairs.'

Coward's crime had been to write a sketch for the stage in which Edith was caricatured under the name of Hernia Whittleblot with her brothers Gob and Sago. When the review appeared Osbert wrote to Coward: 'Insulting my sister is a fine beginning for you. We look forward to other triumphs. Have you tried cheating at cards?'

Why did the Sitwells draw down this controversy on themselves. John Pearson in a mammoth book about Edith, Osbert and Sacheverell (he was a third member of the family also a writer), gives us an opportunity to see the trio in perspective.

The main reason for rows that circled about the Sitwells' heads would seem to be their flair for publicity. They were expert performers as well as writers. In the twenties Osbert and Edith achieved a literary scandal when they presented *Façade,* a recital of Edith's poems set to music by their friend William Walton, and spoken through a megaphone which protruded through a hole in a white front cloth. The critics went to town on this and the Sitwells were immediately established as characters and material for the gossip columns.

They had a real flair for organisation. In 1945 Osbert and Edith managed to stage a Royal poetry reading at Aeolian Hall with the Queen and the two princesses in the front seats. Taking part were 'approved ' poets like Walter De La Mare, W. J. Turner and T. S. Eliot. Shortly after this success Osbert and Edith went to the United States, where they took New York by storm.

Edith, bangled and bejewelled and proclaiming her descent from Queen Elizabeth I, and Osbert, former grenadier and impeccable knight, appealed to a society which had officially rid itself of class distinction but secretly hungered after the trappings of aristocracy. Ten thousand came to listen to the pair in the New York Town Hall and when they restaged *Façade* at the Museum of Modern Art, tickets were sold at what would be in today's money £80 each. Certain people in New York didn't like them. (I remember Oliver Gogarty doing a rather harsh parody of Osbert reciting his poetry shaking like a leaf with Parkinson's disease and John Mason Browne thought them 'the more outrageous sort of English amateur'.) But, on the whole, they made an extraordinary impression in the United States.

In the end of it all, how good were the Sitwells as writers? Mr Pearson in his fascinating book doesn't really answer this question. His artistic judgment in the first place isn't so hot. It is a gross understatement to say of Tchelitchew that he was merely 'a draughtsman of genius'. Robert Nichols may not have been a major poet but he was certainly not 'a charlatan' as Mr Pearson calls him. Ethel Mannin was much more than just 'a gushing lady novelist'.

In so far as he makes a judgment at all, Mr Pearson seems to come down in favour of Edith as the most creative of the two. This is perhaps the popular view. It ignores the remarkable prose of Osbert's autobiographies which capture in a way that no other work in English has done the essence of the English aristocracy at the time of their decline and fall. It is also one of the most hilarious books of the century which may be connected with the fact that the Sitwells had Irish blood through the Hely-Hutchinsons, a fact which Mr Pearson does not pursue, though it might help to explain the pair's flamboyant eccentricity.

Osbert for someone of his class also took very courageous and special stands which were not sufficiently emphasised in the book. Though he had fought in the First World War as an officer in the Grenadiers, half way through the Second one he thought fit to issue a general denunciation of war, an act of courage of the sort which was only equalled among writers living in England by Bernard Shaw.

The truth is that both Osbert and Edith were worth biographies of their own and by putting them together in one book with their brother Sacheverell, Mr Pearson has given us a brilliant picture of Sitwelliana, but has not quite brought off a full portrait of his sitters.

14 January 1979.

3. Yeats Père

A case could be made that the most artistic family of the twentieth century was the Yeats'. Look at the record. William (W. B.) won the Nobel Prize for literature and is looked on by some critics as the greatest poet in English since Shakespeare. Jack was a major European painter of astonishing intellectual range. Their father John Butler Yeats is only just beginning to get the recognition he deserves as a portrait painter. Henry Lamb has called him 'by far the greatest painter Ireland has produced', and Robert Henri, the American art critic, went so far as to say that 'John Butler Yeats is the greatest British portrait painter of the Victorian era'. Now an American scholar, William M. Murphy, has written a biography of the prodigious father of the two Yeats boys, Willie and Jack.

John Butler Yeats was not only one of the great painters of his time but one of the great talkers too. When the young G. K. Chesterton visited the Yeats' house he decided that such talk as came from J. B. Yeats' mouth was no longer possible in England – 'the swift construction of a complicated sentence'.

Fortunately, the father wrote thousands of letters to his son and from these we can gather something of the extraordinary mind that produced the conversation which entranced everyone. John Butler Yeats had views on everything. As an old Trinity College man he thought that the college 'insulted the national soul, and avoided controversy, as a spirit of enquiry would be dangerous for England, and therefore excelled only in mathematics and things scientific.'

John Butler Yeats warned his son against preoccupation with money, telling him that the 'Dublin definition of a gentleman was somebody not wholly interested in getting on in life.' Whenever Willie would appear likely to take up regular employment, this extraordinary father would be on his back, pleading with him not to let anything interfere with the life of the artist. He himself had a small private income but made little money from his painting.

His wife, a Pollexfen, was from a merchant shipping family in Sligo, but John B. Yeats was not in the least embarrassed by the superior wealth of his in-laws. 'I gave a tongue to the sea cliffs,' he said referring to Willie's poetry and his nautical maternal forebears. John B. Yeats never stopped analysing the family traits in his sons. When Willie sent him money once in America, the old boy's comment was, 'It was like a Yeats to send the money and make no fuss about it. It was a Pollexfen to have the money to send.'

Writing to an American friend in 1903, he gave this remarkable summing up of the two traditions in Ireland: 'Given the Protestant efficiency, the Catholic Irishmen would leap to far higher altitudes than the Protestant will ever attain – because of his imagination and traditions. If Catholic Ireland should awake and become articulate, we should all listen, spellbound. Catholic Ireland has something to say or will have something to say, and this whether it fights with its priests or agrees with them.'

John B. Yeats had as keen an insight into writing as he had into painting. When T. S. Eliot read the father's letters to his son he wrote, 'Mr Yeats understands poetry better than anyone else I have ever known who was not a poet and better than most of those who have the reputation of poets.'

He spotted Joyce's *A Portrait of the Artist as a Young Man* long before it became famous: 'Not a sentence, not a line, not a word, I would blot. It mutters and murmurs and sometimes sings. That book will live forever, preserved like a fly in amber by its incomparable style.'

One of the reasons that John B. Yeats never made money in his lifetime was that he was reluctant to finish a painting. He would often spend a year on a portrait. Then if he did not like it he would buy it back from the sitter. Late in life he went to New York and for twenty years became one of the great figures of the city operating out of Petipas Cafe on 23rd Street and 9th Avenue. In New York he found a patron after his own heart, that great Irish/American John Quinn who paid him a weekly sum as a commission to paint a self-portrait. Fifteen years later the self-portrait was unfinished but a masterpiece.

Many people thought that John B. Yeats lacked the stamina to stay at his easel. Now we can see that it was probably the other way around. He had a secret energy which he used to let him live the total life of the artist – doing only what he felt was perfect. In those astonishing portraits in the National Gallery of Ireland we can see the results of that energy, the force of personality crackling off the canvas from a brushwork as delicate as the flutter of butterfly wings.

Dr Murphy has provided delightful insights into the Yeats family in this splendid biography. We see the Yeats sisters Lily and Lolly when they are young trying to get their homework finished in the drawing room while a sound like bees buzzing is humming in the background. It is Willie at his poems. Finally, the girls would say, 'Now Willie, stop composing,' and the young poet would be put into the kitchen, where he could murmur and chant away to his heart's content.

There is a moving account of the old painter in New York reading to a crowd in Petipas Cafe from a copy of Willie's 'Green Helmet' published by Lily and Lolly at the Cuala Press. 'His eyes filled up with tears as he brought it to a finish – his voice fairly crooned the words.'

One can't help wondering as one reads this book, with its record of privation and poverty, did John B. Yeats in his determination to have his sons live their lives on an imaginative rather than a materialistic level, do injury to any of them.

Fanatic devotion to religion (and to John B. Yeats art was a religion) can damage families. It is possible that John B. Yeats' wife Susan may have suffered by the family's disinterest in material things. She is a shadowy figure in the book: for the last years of her life she was crippled by a stroke. Sad, that she should never have shared in her sons' glory.

22 April 1979.

4. Dance Time

Richard Buckle has now published the second volume of his autobiography, *In the Wake of Diaghilev.* Dickie Buckle became a magic name to me in, of all places, the Dublin Law Library when, as a very young barrister, a chum in the next seat introduced me to Buckle's writing, and we would talk of ballet, the Golden Age singers, and the latest L.P. of Solemses Gregorian, in between waiting for the briefs that in those pre-Second Programme days were often hard to come by.

Dickie Buckle's ballet writing was the only work available in English at that time which captured the allure of this most romantic of arts. He has a real gift for a character sketch – and with his English whimsy captures the butterfly personalities of the great dancers as they flit before the eye. In 1954 a chance came to meet this paragon. He had arranged what was said to be the greatest exhibition of Diaghilev's memorabilia in the world at the Edinburgh Festival and would be there in person during the last three weeks of August. I got my expenses to Edinburgh by arranging to pole vault on the Isle of Bute at the Highland Games (about three hours journey by boat and train from the Scottish capital) and one night after a ravishing performance of *Romeo and Juliet* by the Royal Danish Ballet I met the man himself. He talked quite as well as he wrote, wasn't a bit snobbish about discussing ballet with a tough (he had served in the Grenadiers during the war at Anzio) and promised to come to Dublin which he did but for too short a time.

Ballet was all for some years after; and Dublin, through the enterprise of Stanley Illsley and Leo McCabe had some of the world's greatest dancers at the Olympia –

Yvette Chauviré, Alicia Markova, Jean Babileé, John Gilpin and the incredible Eric Bruhn, so one had an opportunity to see first class dancing at home for a while. Then in Sweden, through Dickie, I met Vera Volkova, the last standard bearer of the art of *epaulément,* who persuaded me to take dancing classes with the Royal Swedish Ballet which, at that time, had Gerd Anderson and Marion Orlando in the company. I even wrote a ballet libretto of Synge's *The Playboy of the Western World* which was to be choreographed by Ivo Cramer but which was shelved because the composer, Hugo Alfven, died before he got going on the score.

To read another instalment of Dickie Buckle's life then is for me, I have to confess, a voyage into a world of enchantment which no other autobiography can create for me. With much affection and exquisite cunning he cultivated the friendships of some of the great dancers of the Golden Age – Lydia Lopokova, Tamara Karsavina, Lydia Sokolova, and extracted from them memories of Diaghilev, Fokine, Pavlova, Nijinsky, priceless pearls of ballet history which would have perished had it not been for his industry. He was an ideal companion for these old tabbies, sympathetic, sensitive, a surrogate son in whose fascinated ear they poured their precious tales.

He tells us here how Karsavina maintained that *epaulément,* that angling of head and shoulder, in relation to torso and legs, was never mastered by English dancers. Buckle agrees and maintains that the Russians danced with the whole body, the British did not.

But it shouldn't be thought that this book is all about the past. There's an enthralling account of Rudolf Nureyev here. Who could catch the essence of the Russian dancer's personality better than Buckle as he says goodnight to Rudi at 2 a.m. after a ferocious day of ballet classes and bustle. 'When he showed me politely to the door I realised he was going for a walk. This pampered pussy, surrounded by courtiers, became in the early hours a cat that walked by himself.'

When he visits Moscow Buckle catches in his fine prose the essence of that strange city with its history of Czar and Commissar. 'I woke at 3.15 to hear a swishing sound on the cobbled plain outside my window. It was being washed. Soon after dawn there came a subdued roll of kettle drums and I rushed to the window. A company of soldiers were diagonalling past the equestrian statue of Nicolas I. In their long grey greatcoats they marched in an easy, slouching, democratic way which I found charming.'

Buckle is somewhat of a rebel against the British ballet establishment. He does give credit where credit is due to Ninette de Valois but refers somewhat cattily to 'the tentacles of her swelling enterprise', and describes her as 'combining the self assurance of Queen Victoria with the doggedness of Florence Nightingale'.

One senses that with all her powers of organisation Ninette, in Dickie Buckle's eyes, lacks that ultimate flair which can bring fire and lightning on the stage. Another British ballet figure, Anton Dolin, also comes off badly in the breach when Buckle sends his darts in. There is, too, an excruciating funny story of Serge Lifar at the Metropolitan Museum in New York trying to grab the cameras for his ageing profile before George Balanchine arrived.

A true Londoner, Dickie Buckle lives in a flat in Covent Garden. It is eighty-two steps up and he would throw you down the key from the top window to let yourself in. He tells us here that Tamara Karsavina used to arrive breathless at the top of the steps to get on with the biography he was doing of her. She was then over eighty. That this queen of dancers would traipse up eighty-two steps, to tell her story to Dickie Buckle, is perhaps the finest tribute that could be paid to him, as a writer about this most romantic of arts.

22 May 1983

5. Patrick Kavanagh

In 1948 the American Olympic team came to Dublin and competed at College Park. I remember in the pavilion seeing a fellow talking to Bob Richards, the Olympic pole vault champion. Afterwards Richards told me that this man was a famous Irish poet. I'd seen this particular chap scratching himself and muttering to himself in buses and I told Richards he had been taken for a ride. Later I found out that the fellow was Paddy Kavanagh, Ireland's greatest poet since Yeats, who was writing articles on sport in the *Irish Press* under a pseudonym. When I got to know him later Kavanagh would greet me with a whinny of triumph in Grafton Street and tell me the latest height someone I was going to compete against in the pole vault from America or England had jumped. When the fibre glass pole came in he was fit to be tied, rubbing his hands and whinnying: 'I saw them using it in the White City. You're finished. They're in orbit now. It's not a jump. It's a catapult.'

It was said that Kavanagh didn't praise others. He couldn't – his standards were too high and he didn't tell lies about art. It was the dilemma of a real artist in a small bohemian society that thrived on mutual flattery. But he was receptive to praise himself. Once I wrote a review of the stage version of *Tarry Flynn* in the London *Times* and he made a point of telling me he thought it was generous. I was glad, because Kavanagh died not long after, while *Tarry Flynn* was playing in his capital of Dundalk.

Now Peter Kavanagh, his brother has written a biography of Patrick Kavanagh. There are two types of biography – one which gives you all the facts and you make what you can of them, and the other which gives you the facts in such a way as to create a living picture of the person written about. There is much about Kavanagh that is not in this book but in a way this is the work of an artist who has trapped something of the imaginative soul of his subject in a book.

Peter says he has only a hazy memory of how his brother looked: 'His physical appearance has scarcely registered on my memory. When we met we recognised each other, not by appearance but in some manner difficult to describe, perhaps in the same way animals recognise their own kind.'

But one day as he was writing this book, Patrick, who had been dead ten years, appeared before Peter and he had a good look at him for the purpose of the biography. I have no difficulty in accepting this. Peter was indeed his brother's keeper. Like Stanislaus Joyce and his brother James, Peter devoted his life to keeping the flame of Patrick's genius alive. When they were boys on the farm in Monaghan, Patrick used to say the Rosary before climbing into bed and then check the top button of Peter's shirt to make sure it was open and there was no danger of his choking. They remained that close throughout.

In Dublin in the forties it was Peter who paid most of the bills. The brothers used to meet three times a day for meals, once in a restaurant at Westland Row and twice in a flat where they cooked their own food. After that they'd meet late in the evening and walk home along the docks, commenting on the foreign ships and cargoes.

Patrick couldn't get work as a writer, no matter how he tried. He applied for a script-writer's job in Radio Éireann as late as 1947 and didn't even get an interview. Thinking then that Seán McEntee, having written a book of verse, might be sympathetic to him, Patrick wrote but did no better than with the public servants in Radio Éireann. Strangely enough his only fan with enough muscle to get him a job was Archbishop Gilmartin of Tuam, who virtually insisted that Patrick get a job on the *Catholic Standard*. Here he was a terrific success as a feature writer and film critic, under a great editor, Peter O'Curry, who gave him as much freedom as he wanted. Later on John Costello, SC, who had cross-examined Patrick severely in a libel action saw to it that he got an extern lectureship in University College, Dublin. Peter relates the well-known story about Costello meeting Kavanagh at the polling booth, but omits what must have been one of the great replies in legal history when Costello said to Kavanagh in cross-examination during the trial: 'But I am only quoting your own words, Mr Kavanagh.' The poet replied, 'The Devil can cite scripture for his purpose.'

Peter includes a fair lot of warts in this biography. In 1949 Patrick sold a farm without telling his brother, who had an equal right to it. As Peter says: 'It was one of the mean acts of which he was capable.'

Patrick often sold books to two publishers at the one time but there was nothing strange about that. Among Irish writers then the principle was to get the cheque in your hand first and worry afterwards. But Peter is off-beam when he says that Patrick never used bad language or blasphemy or indulged in rabelaisian talk. This is nonsense. I have heard Patrick Kavanagh screeching the holy name across pubs, and the trend of his conversation at times would have made Hugh Heffner get up and run.

It's not necessary to be poor to be a poet. But if you're poor, being a poet can be a hard station. Baudelaire, Verlaine, Edgar Alan Poe are examples and Kavanagh was in that tradition. He was harried from pillar to post and never knew the luxury of having enough money to live on.

'Art is life squeezed through a repression,' was one of his sayings and it is easy to see how it applied to his case. But he emerged from catastrophies with renewed strength as a poet. After his operation for cancer of the lung in 1954 he produced the magnificent 'Come dance with Kitty Stobling', with its astonishing sonnet sequence, probably among the finest sonnets in the English language of our time.

Peter has raised a monument to his brother. It is not the final one, but a good one to be going on with.

9 March 1980

6. Waugh Games

I dined with Evelyn Waugh in the Kildare Street Club in 1956. He was good company. I talked about boxing and he told me about his parachute jumping. Apart from squashing one of the other gentlemen present, who had a voice like a mouse scraping on a window and who wanted to talk about Graham Greene, I noticed no trace of savagery in Mr Waugh.

But these letters! In *The Letters of Evelyn Waugh* edited by Mark Amory, he lashes out with a tongue as venomous as a caged rattlesnake. He describes Proust as 'mentally defective' and states that Picasso's painting 'can only be treated as crooners are by their devotees'. The brave Protestant Pastor Niemoller, who survived Hitler's death camps, is dismissed as 'a seedy kind of clergyman – just flat stupid and boring.' Winston Churchill was, according to Waugh, 'always in the wrong, always surrounded by crooks, a most unsuccessful father – simply a "Radio Personality" who outlived his prime. "Rallied the nation" indeed! I was a serving soldier in 1940. How we despised his orations.'

No one loved a lord as dearly as Waugh did. The English caste system makes people sit up and beg like performing dogs, and Waugh from a very clearly-defined middle class background did his tricks in order to keep in with the most ancient families. Some of the most revered were Catholics, so it didn't hurt that Waugh had become one himself and was able to combine his lust for ritual with a comfortable sense of continuity. This, of course, meant disdaining any association with the native Irish, whose presence in England as servants and labourers has always been an embarrassment to the old

Catholics there. 'You have no conception,' he wrote to Nancy Mitford, 'of the Irish mole-like malice. Detraction is their passion. You should have heard the wireless programme commemorating the centenary of George Moore's birthday. They had been at work on it for years collecting reports from everyone who had ever known him from the groom at Moore Park to Dublin literary colleagues. One after another the cracked old Irish voices took up the tale for nearly two hours, each demolishing bit by bit every corner of his reputation. That was Ireland all right.'

Waugh had ideas about coming to live in Ireland and buying Lord Gormanston's house in Co Meath, but changed his mind. 'Darling Nancy,' he wrote again to Nancy Mitford, 'among the countless blessings I thank God for, my failure to find a house in Ireland comes first. The peasants are malevolent. All their smiles are false as hell. Their priests are very suitable for them but not for foreigners. No coal at all. Awful incompetence everywhere. No native capable of doing the simplest job properly. No schools for children.'

Is it any wonder that J. B. Priestly thought Waugh had gone mad, in trying to ape the manners of a country gentleman? It is hard to defend the sheer malice of a letter like this one to Ann Fleming about the death of our own Lord Longford of the Gate Theatre: 'Our best news is Edward Longford's death. Before the body was cold (his brother) Frank (Pakenham) was telephoning all over the United Kingdom trying to promote publicity. He persuaded me to write a panegyric in *The Observer*. It was a model of how such a thing should be done so as not to offend the family and at the same time reveal the essential absurdity of the deceased.'

The deceased was, in fact, a first-rate playwright, a scholar, a patron of the arts, an Irish Republican and an exquisite translator of Gaelic verse but he didn't move in the correct London set so he gets Waugh's trowel on his coffin clay. How untrue the allegation is that Frank

Pakenham was hustling obituaries for his late brother can be seen from the fact that I wrote Edward Longford's obituary in the London *Times* and I certainly was not approached by Frank Pakenham to do so. Another reference to the Longford family is worth a chuckle though, Waugh's malice at its lightest (the Meg referred to is Waugh's daughter and the Lord Longford is Frank Pakenham who succeeded his brother and who had just been involved in producing a report against pornography): 'On a Friday passing through London I was feeding Meg on caviar and what should I see at the next table but Antonia Fraser eating grouse. But she gave birth next day, so I suppose was free of abstinence. Her mama's book on Queen Victoria was jolly good. It is a great relief her papa (Lord Longford) is not home secretary – else we should all be murdered by sexual maniacs.'

The violent prejudices and incurable snobbery of these letters should not be allowed to obscure the fact that they were written by a man whose serious work will survive. Evelyn Waugh is one of the great satirists in the English language. He heard the shrieking rip as the fabric of the British empire came apart and when it finally collapsed he had the characters of the time caught in between the covers of his novels. With the empire gone and the class system in decline, there was nothing left for him in the end. Even the beloved ritual of the church he had joined had gone: 'Easter used to mean so much to me,' he wrote to Diana Mosley, 'before Pope John and his Council. They destroyed the beauty of the liturgy. I have not yet soaked myself in petrol and gone up in flames but I now cling to the faith doggedly without joy.'

He died on Easter Day in 1966. For some years before, according to these letters, he had been drinking a bottle of whiskey a day, a bottle of paraldehyde a week along with sleeping pills and other aids to escape from misery.

21 December 1980

7. James Stephens – Storyteller

James Stephens was one of those Irish writers who had the double gift – he was a great entertainer as well as a great writer. For the last twenty years of his life he spent long periods sitting on a stool in BBC studios charming the English nation with tales about dogs, women and fairies, told in a voice that was probably unique in the history of broadcasting, with the siren lure of its sound. This got him a reputation as a sort of delightful Irish leprechaun when all the time what was sitting on the stool was a tortured piece of humanity who had gazed on the human condition with a clear eye and come back with a not very optimistic view of it.

Now, Dr Gus Martin has published for the first time a selection of James Stephens' short stories which shows us the other side of this extraordinary man's nature. These tales strip away layer by layer the various skins by which we protect ourselves from life, till we are confronted by our own nature in the raw. 'Schoolfellows' is a terrifying story about a cadger who waylays an amiable old school friend each evening to borrow half-crowns, till the friend finally revolts and punches him.

'And every time I saw him after that I ran.'

You feel as if some tribal Irish law has been broken, which most of us are afraid to confront lest we be devoured by the vengeance of the gods.

In 'Three Young Wives' a woman is going to have a child and she becomes afraid that her husband wishes her to die in childbirth. In his face one day she has glimpsed such a look, after she contracted smallpox from another child and her beauty had vanished overnight. How many of us harbour such secret thoughts but will not admit them to the outer level of consciousness.

'The Triangle' is about a married couple who lead lives of quiet desperation till a woman lodger supplies the goad of jealousy, which gives a new meaning to their empty lives.

Very often these stories have no dialogue. They just tell what happened in spare, terrible prose which can raise the hair on the back of your neck. People die very often in them. But who will claim immortality under the present dispensation of providence!

'Hunger' is one such tale. If St Vincent de Paul, General Booth and Lenin arrived on the same platform at the one time to denounce poverty they could hardly make more of an impact than Stephens' stark description of how a Dublin family was to be devoured by the social system of the time. His technique is unique, almost as if Dostoyevsky had managed to compress an existential view of man into five pages instead of a massive novel. The art is concealed. But occasionally you glimpse the sculptor of words at work under the raw prose: 'He listened to the voluble Parisians who went by speaking in a haste so breathless that he marvelled how the prepositions and conjunctions stuck to their duty in so swirling an emotion of chatter.' And: 'Nothing is true forever. A man and a fact will become equally decrepit and will tumble in the same ditch, but truth is as mortal as man, and both are outlived by the tortoise and the crow.'

When James Joyce met James Stephens he told him his knowledge of Irish life was 'non-Catholic and so non-existent'.

But Stephens could have replied that these stories were not about Irish life but about human nature, men and women living without crutches in that state of siege in which man lives with his fellow man.

One more thing. Don't be disappointed by the lack of

story in these tales. You will find something else there if you wish to seek it – yourself.

22 March 1981

8. Joycespeak

'When Mullocky won the couple of colds' has a familiar ring about it. If you know your Tom Moore you'll think of *When Malachy wore the collar of gold.*

'I met with dapper dandy and he shocked me big the hamd' is easy to spot for everyone knows the second verse of *The Wearin' of the Green.* But try this one, 'turn agate, wedding-town, laud men of Londub'. It takes a lot of teasing of the mind to see that this refers to 'Turn again, Whittington, Lord Mayor of London'.

Such clever puns. Brilliant. Sustained through 600 pages of *Finnegans Wake* by James Joyce. He wanted to write a book about sleep, having exhausted the waking state in his other works. So he created a Universal Figure who lies with his head in Howth and his feet in Castleknock. Through his mind flows the consciousness of Ireland and all the world, 'though dev do espart' ('till death do us part) and 'Humphrey Chimpden Earwicker' (Here Comes Everybody) dissolves into the eternal all-embracing sea. There are the names of over 700 rivers in *Finnegans Wake,* all related distantly to our own Anna Livia, and their dulcet sounds cascade in and out of the bizarre language of the book. It isn't just written in one tongue – Norwegian, Danish, German, French, Italian, Russian, Sanskrit occur. How can the average bloke who takes up the book know what is going on? The answer is he can't – without help.

Now Roland McHugh gives us *Annotations to Finnegans Wake* which goes through the book word by word and gives us detailed explanations to even the smallest reference. What Mr McHugh has done is to correlate all the books on *Finnegans Wake,* with additional information provided by himself and others who have worked with him, and bring the lot together in one book. This wonderful encyclopaedia is the only one which can bring *Finnegans Wake* within the reach of the ordinary reader. One is constantly astounded at the range of Mr McHugh's knowledge. Time and time again I hurried to his annotations to see if he had slipped up (after all Mr McHugh didn't grow up in Ireland so he could have been excused for missing some of Joyce's more obscure references, especially in regard to songs), but each time he comes up trumps.

'The grinning statesmen, Brock and Leon, have shunted the grumbling coundedtouts, Starlin and Ser Artur Ghinis.' This one is really tough. But it means a lot more when you look at Mr McHugh's note that Joyce's father was Secretary of the United Liberal Club in Dublin during the 1880 general election, and the Liberal candidates were Maurice Brookes and Dr Robert Dyer Lyons who ousted Sir Arthur Guinness and James Stirling.

Mr McHugh does miss a few. 'Perihelygangs' is a reference to Tim Healy who betrayed Parnell and whose followers were known as the Healy Gang, a fact that Mr McHugh has missed out on, even though on the same page there is a reference to Healy's lieutenant, Joe Biggar. Nor does he relate 'Goalball I've struck this daylit dielate night of nights, by golly!' to Callanan's 'Convict of Clonmel'. He is wrong about Landsdowne Road rugby club being built in Beggars Bush and about J. B. Dunlop inventing the rubber tyre (it was the pneumatic tyre). But these are small mistakes in a work of titanic industry. There is no excuse now for people to be mystified by *Finnegans Wake*. Mr McHugh has unravelled it for us. The question that is being asked now that we have an opportunity to grasp its word meanings is, is it valid as a work of art? Was Joyce so far in front of his time that only now can we begin to see what he was at, or did he go out of his tree altogether and start talking gobbldygook? Once when I was young an elderly barrister friend who was at Belvedere with Joyce told me about meeting the great man in Paris after an international rugby match between Ireland and France and later discovering references to the same match in *Finnegans Wake* (Mr McHugh might possibly have credited me with the information that I was the first to decipher Joyce's rugby references). Samuel Beckett has told about Joyce forbidding him, when he was taking dictation from him, to cross out the words 'come in' which were not part of the intended text, but had been said by Joyce to someone knocking at the door without Beckett hearing it. Joyce's justification for this extraordinary direction was 'It happened.'

Is this art? We must ask ourselves the question.

Mr McHugh's unparalleled work has given us an admirable opportunity to answer it.

19 October 1980

9. Harold Nicolson

She was a beautiful lesbian who dressed in riding trousers and was liable to run off with the next woman she met. He was a confirmed homosexual who thought that 'lust is a noble thing' and chased any dishy male that came into his ken. After they married he became advisor to prime ministers and kings, while she became a well-known poetess whose poems are in *The Oxford Book of Modern Verse*. Now James Lees-Milne in *Harold Nicolson: A Biography 1886-1929* gives us an account of Harold Nicolson who was the husband in this extraordinary menage. Husband? Is this a fair description? Well, Nicolson fathered two sons, Ben and Nigel and they grew up as fulfilled and successful human beings.

Mr Lees-Milne has very cleverly in this biography (which, alas, only takes us halfway through Nicolson's life, there's more to come) depicted the international political scene against which the episodes of Harold Nicolson's private life are played out. While he was trying to keep Lloyd George from strangling Clemenceau (literally, according to the author) at the Peace Conference, and scurrying between Balfour and Poincaré who were deciding the future of Europe, Harold Nicolson was receiving daily bulletins on his wife's carry-on. She had run away with a beautiful London debutante, Violet Keppel and was trying to stop Violet's marriage to a handsome (male) war-hero, Major Denys Trefussis, MC. Harold, meanwhile, in between Foreign Office Communiqués, seems not to have been averse to knocking off any bit of male trade that came his way.

After Versailles, Harold Nicolson went to Persia as

first counsellor. While he was engaged there in making sure that Britain could grab the best part of the world's oil wealth, his wife fell for Virginia Woolf. He was hardly back in England than she was out of this one and chasing Mary Campbell (the beautiful wife of the poet Roy Campbell) and about to publish a set of scandalous verses. In the meantime the indomitable Harold had chummed up with the young critic Raymond Mortimer so he had a convenient shoulder to lay his burning brow on. As well, he had become a writer in his own right with the production of his semi-fictional work (*Some People*) and successful biographies of Tennyson and Swinburne.

Mr Lees-Milne's astonishing proposition is that Harold Nicolson and Victoria Sackville-West loved each other with a gem-like flame that makes Dante and Beatrice look like transient flirts. This may not be as preposterous as it sounds. The letters of the two certainly show devotion that is not always apparent in more stable marriages. They seem to have been miserable when they were parted from one another. The curious thing is that despite their bizarre life styles, the Nicolsons' 'story' is an argument against divorce. After all, when society would have liked to have parted them from each other because of their unusual tastes, they insisted on staying together and as they grew old they turned into model examples of a happy couple.

As one reads the book, though, more and more nasty things emerge about Harold Nicolson. He had unpleasant racist ideas, for instance: 'Take beastly niggers to F.O. and round by Tower to see London' is how this foreign office diplomat describes escorting two Haitian diplomats to King Edward VII's funeral. There are frequent references in his diaries to 'oily Jews'. He was delighted when his club, Bucks, expelled Eddie Knoblock for having entertained Charlie Chaplin to lunch. When his son Nigel became a war major and received the MBE and Harold and Vita became Sir Harold and Lady Nicolson, they were snobbish enough to dislike both honours as they considered they would have to share them with middle class officers and city mayors and mayoresses. His prejudice intruded on his literary judgment. He told Osbert Sitwell that he and Eliot had 'uninteresting minds'.

What sort of a louser is he at all, one thinks, as the book proceeds. Yet it is clear that Harold Nicolson was free from one vice – the greatest British one of all – hypocrisy. He was ashamed of nothing except to be ashamed. He let it all hang out in those famous diaries, which went on into the sixties and exposed the double-dealing of the society he was born into.

As we leave him in the first volume, having resigned from the foreign office to become a writer, we should remember what was to come: the passionate liberal who would represent National Labour in the House of Commons, the causes he later championed, the loyalties he refused to abandon. Faithful in a fashion to himself.

7 December 1980

10. Lady Gregory

Serge Diaghilev who created the modern Russian ballet, is generally held to have been the greatest organiser of the arts in this century. Our own Lady Gregory, who more than anyone else kept the Abbey alive during its difficult early years, provides a good challenge to Diaghilev. In some ways she is ahead of the Russian. Diaghilev never actually created any ballets himself: he brought people of genius together who worked under him and produced masterpieces. But Lady Gregory herself wrote plays for the Abbey, some of them little masterpieces like *The Rising of the Moon, The Workhouse Ward, The Gaol Gate*. But writing plays was a secondary consideration for this remarkable woman. Her first aim was to create a National Theatre that would make its mark in the world. Lady Gregory was a masterful woman, ruthless about paying debts, cutting salaries and sacking those she felt didn't fit in with the Gregory plan for keeping the Abbey going. She had the rarest of gifts in Ireland, an ability to devote her energies to a cause over a long period without being disheartened by setbacks and failures. She had an astonishing flair for spotting new playwrights and actors which is all the more remarkable since she didn't come to work in the theatre until she was fifty-two.

Now Daniel J. Murphy has edited her journals which deal with the years from 1916-23. They provide an intriguing record of Irish artistic and political life during these important years. It is clear from the journals that this titled woman had adopted a Republican stance at a time when the majority of her class were fanatically in favour of the union with Great Britain. This wasn't just a reaction on Lady Gregory's part from her background. As a child, inspired by her nurse Mary Sheridan, Augusta Gregory had saved her money to buy Fenian pamphlets across the post office counter in the village near her mansion.

In her journal for October 1921 we read of her pleasure that Kevin Barry's own company want to present her play *The Rising of The Moon* in the Queen's Theatre in aid of victims of the Black and Tans. She admired Michael Collins greatly and was proud that he made a point to come into the Abbey regularly when he was on the run – 'Always with a strong bodyguard around him.' She notes that one of the nuns at Gort commented to her, 'It was you Lady Gregory who was the first to bring Irish to this neighbourhood' – this refers to her activities with the Gaelic League.

Lady Gregory's nationalism, however, was of a kind that didn't shirk criticising her own countrymen when she thought it necessary. She fought like a tiger for Synge's *Playboy* when pious nationalists tried to have it taken off the Abbey stage, and later for O'Casey when the same gang attacked *The Plough and the Stars*.

In America, when the Abbey was on tour, she was equally firm with the Irish-American groups that tried to attack the performances. J. M. Kerrigan told me once that he was acting in *The Playboy* in Philadelphia when there was a riot in the audience. He heard a whisper from behind the stage prop: 'Go easy, we are going to start all over again after the interval.' It was Lady Gregory who had crept on the stage to issue the instructions. And rightwell this determined little lady insisted on taking the curtain down and starting the play all over again. Contrary to what is sometimes said about her, Lady Gregory had a very keen sense of dramatic construction. We read in her journal for May 1923 of Shaw reading to her the scene of the relief of Orleans from his play *St Joan*. As Shaw read the play the long-awaited change in the wind was indicated by the waving of a pennant. Lady

Gregory suggested to Shaw that it would be more dramatic to have the page boy sneeze and was later delighted to note that Shaw had adopted her suggestion and used it in the play.

Lady Gregory used always to travel third class, stay in lodgings instead of hotels and take her lunches in Lyons Corner House when she was in London in order to save money for her beloved Abbey. She worked unceasingly for her various causes, the return of the Lane Pictures to Ireland, keeping Coole going as a country house, obtaining the release of an Egyptian patriot. She was a busy little woman who seemed to have the most extraordinary entrées to the leading political figures in England. She even succeeded in winning over Carson, the Ulster leader, to the cause of having the Lane Pictures returned to Dublin, though she must have been a trifle offended when he asked her did Hugh Lane paint all of the pictures or only some of them.

In between all this she composed menus for Yeats to keep his health up, mothered O'Casey at Coole, was a splendid housekeeper and devoted a lot of her time to her grandchildren, 'the chicks' as she refers to them constantly in these journals.

Lady Gregory combined two rare qualities. She was a dynamic woman of genius who had a deep streak of compassion in her. She ranks among the persons of genius produced in Europe this century.

In 1942 Galway County Council levelled Lady Gregory's house at Coole.

Wood Quay wasn't born yesterday.

28 January 1979

11. John Masefield

When John Masefield became Poet Laureate of England in 1930 it was a popular appointment. Masefield was a poet who had an affinity with the ordinary man, and who had never been to a university but had served both before the mast and behind a bar. The irony, however, is that although he was to hold the post for thirty-nine years, Masefield was past his peak when he became Poet Laureate. The poems he is remembered most for today were nearly all written before 1914. It is only necessary, of course, to have written one real poem to become immortal. Masefield's poem beginning 'I must go down to the sea' has secured him that position. But why in the course of a long and productive life should he have written so little that was touched with fire? Now Constance Babington Smith has given us a thoroughly-researched biography of Masefield (written with family approval). But she does not pose or answer the questions of the drying-up of Masefield's poetic power.

She gives us an absorbing account of Masefield's early life, the suffering he endured through a tyrannical step-mother and feckless solicitor-father, and his adventures sailing before the mast when he graduated from the Conway Training Ship. At seventeen years of age Masefield gave up life at sea for a while and became a barman in New York, where he was befriended by an Irishman, Luke O'Connor, who owned the Columbian Tavern at Greenwich Corner. Masefield seems to have been helped by a lot of Irishmen. It was Yeats who first encouraged him to continue as a poet and invited the young Masefield to his Monday evenings in Woburn Place, in London. 'You are my father and grandfather,' Masefield wrote later to Yeats. And he was to remember his friend as having 'a face unlike any else in the world – vivid with wit'. Then one night Yeats brought Synge along to read his play *Riders to the Sea* and from him Masefield learned to look for themes 'That come out of life' and not from the dull plains of the intellect. It was for his poems, written between the time he met Yeats and the outbreak of the Great War, that Masefield is best remembered. On the eve of the war he wrote almost in valediction to his poetic gift an ode to those English soldiers who:

knew the misery of the soaking trench
The freezing in the rigging, the despair
In the revolting second of the wrench
When the blind soul is flung upon the air.

Masefield served as an orderly in ambulance units at various times during the war. It could be thought that a man as highly strung as he was and sensitive, could have had his mind turned by the suffering he encountered among the wounded. Certainly it was out of character that he should have lent his pen to writing a history of the 'Gallipoli Landings' where the Tenth Irish Division and the Anzacs were massacred because of the criminal stupidity of the British high command. In his book Masefield compares the general in charge, Sir Iain Hamilton, (who in fact made a fearful mess of the affair) with Roland at Roncevauz instead of placing him where he belonged with the dedicated blockheads of the General Staff who sacrificed millions of lives by their blundering strategy from 1914 to 1918. Shortly after the war Masefield did write an interesting narrative poem 'Reynard the Fox'. But though he poured out novels and plays, his gift for verse seems to have deserted him. One would have liked more elaboration here and there in this book. Masefield was married to a woman eleven-and-a half years older than himself, who after their marriage spent most of her time with a sinister spinster named

Isobel Fry, who seems to have demanded from her the all-embracing devotion that Alice B. Toklas looked for from Gertrude Stein. The nature of this rum *ménage-à-trois* is not treated in detail in Miss Babington Smith's biography. Then I cannot make out for the life of me what she is trying to imply about Masefield's son or what on earth she means when she writes darkly about Masefield's departure from Pinbury in 1939, 'Some say that they were asked to leave.'

A poet's life, and Masefield was a genuine poet, has darkness as well as light. Miss Babington Smith, although she has given us a thoroughly-researched biography, has not done her subject any favours by glossing over that part of his life when he seems to have walked in the valley of despair.

21 January 1979

12. The Famine

Cecil Woodham-Smith once told me that after she had written her classic on the Famine, *The Great Hunger*, an English duchess came up to her and said: 'Thank you for writing such a wonderful book. We never knew until now why the Irish were so disloyal.'

Because she had written definitive books on Florence Nightingale and Queen Victoria, Mrs Woodham-Smith had a hot line to the English upper classes who were always prepared to listen to what she had to say. The value of her book on the Famine can never be over-estimated.

What Mrs Woodham-Smith does is to present the facts in a sober, detached way. Thus tabled, they are as damning an indictment of British government in Ireland as has ever appeared. According to Mrs Woodham-Smith, Ireland lost two and a half million people from 1845 to 1849. She breaks this down to show that one million died from hunger, a large number from typhus or cholera and the rest emigrated. While the poor died on the roadside because of the potato blight, great cartloads of grain and wheat trundled by for export to Europe. Landlords (though there were exceptions) throughout the country evicted tenants from their cottages for non-payment of rent, so that whole families sometimes froze to death before having the opportunity to die from starvation. In the west many people were driven to live in bogholes which they roofed over with wood like African troglodytes. Every day waggonloads of orphans arrived at the workhouses, to be turned away to die as there was no room for them.

Faced with this catastrophe, the English government

in Mrs Woodham-Smith's words were afraid of 'corrupting the Irish people by kindness and so stifling the virtues of self-reliance and industry'. Charles Edward Trevalyan, the head of the Treasury and in effect in control of the Irish situation, was determined not to interfere with the machinery of private enterprise by giving away free food. 'If the Irish find,' he wrote, 'that there are circumstances in which they can get free government grants we should have a system of mendicity such as the world never saw.'

An economist of the time told Benjamin Jowett, the celebrated Master of Balliol, that he believed 'that the Irish famine would not kill more than a million people and that would scarcely be enough to do much good.' All this has a contemporary ring. One can hear the voice of the toothbrush-moustached Nazi dictator as he instructed his lieutenants to exterminate what he regarded as an inferior race. Admittedly, Trevalyan and his colleagues in the Treasury did not construct the awful engines of destruction that the Nazis did. There was no need to, the famine did it for them. But running through the whole philosophy, as brilliantly elucidated by Mrs Woodham-Smith in this book, is a terrifying proposition whereby man-made principles of economy are set above the survival of human beings. Well might Trevalyan read his bible in sonorous voice while signing the death warrants of a million Irish. Did not the other leader in our time invoke God's blessing as he sanctioned the construction of crematoriums whose existence dishonoured our European heritage?

There are certain questions which are still not answered by Mrs Woodham-Smith in relation to the Famine. Why, for instance, did the Irish not eat fish when the potato crop failed? After all, there were the richest fisheries in Europe on our shores. Mrs Woodham-Smith says that currachs could not handle nets in deep-sea fishing. I asked a currach fisherman about this and he told me it was nonsense. She also says that the fish lay many miles out to sea in forty fathoms of water, which was not so. Even if they were inaccessible to ordinary boats, what about the inland rivers filled with trout, salmon, perch and pike? Why did the people not rebel when they saw the grain leaving the country? True, in Mayo six landlords were killed in the autumn and winter of 1847, but the only resistance was Smith O'Brien's pathetic gesture at Ballingarry.

No: like the Jews going stoically to the gas ovens, it seems there was an element in the Irish character which accepted annihilation as the will of God, and an inertia which made it easier to greet Sergeant Death than to avoid him.

It is most appropriate that Hamish Hamilton should bring out Mrs Woodham-Smith's book at a time when the relations between our two countries are due for re-examination. Before she comes over to negotiate with the Taoiseach, Mrs Thatcher might well refresh her mind with this book and particularly with what Sidney Smith, the celebrated writer and wit wrote about his fellow countrymen 150 years ago: 'The moment the very name of Ireland is mentioned the English seem to bid adieu to common feeling, common prudence and common sense, and to act with the barbarity of tyrants and the fatuity of idiots.'

30 November 1980

13. F. E. Smith – Lord Birkenhead

F. E. Smith was made Lord Chancellor of England when he was forty-six, the youngest since Judge Jeffries in 1685. He had fought his way to leadership of the bar by way of grammar rather than public school and combined a powerful brain and incredible cheek. Once when he was asked by a judge, 'What do you suppose I am on the Bench for?'

F. E. replied, 'It is not for me, your Honour, to attempt to fathom the inscrutable workings of Providence.'

When he became Lord Chancellor his heavy drinking, incessant cigar smoking and eccentric tennis-playing led many of his critics to think that he would demean the office once occupied by Beckett, Wolsey and More. But this extraordinary man was to hand down some of the great judgments in modern legal history, including the famous *Bourne v. Keane* which established bequests for masses for the dead as a legal charity. The beautiful rhythmic prose in which he encased his pronouncements makes them a delight to read, even to those not especially interested in the arguments they expound.

While F. E. adorned the woolsack he was not above letting the buccaneer side of his personality surface if he had dined well. One night, after a High Table at Oxford, he challenged the Olympic miler, W. R. Milligan, to a race in which the Lord Chancellor would run four laps of Tom Quad while Milligan would run eight. F. E., attired in evening clothes and with a dashing buttonhole, completed his fourth lap just as Milligan was finishing his sixth. He was forty-seven at the time.

F. E. Smith, or Lord Birkenhead as he was to become, was a legend in this country when I grew up, because of his associations with the Irish Treaty. One heard tales of him everywhere, especially from W. T. Cosgrave, the first President of the Irish Free State. Once F. E. was invited over to Trinity College to speak at a debate there. A warning was issued to him by an armed group that if he came over he would be assassinated. F. E. arrived off the mail-boat, smoking a large cigar: he refused a bodyguard and, to show his contempt for his purported assailants, went for a walk in the Phoenix Park, a location that hardly had congenial memories for English politicians on visits to Ireland.

Now John Campbell has written a massive biography (eight hundred and thirty-seven pages) of this unusual Englishman.

From an Irish point of view the interest of the book is how Birkenhead turned from being a fanatical supporter of Orangeism to lending his energies towards bringing self-government to Ireland. He had been Carson's 'Galloper' in 1912 and had joined with the Ulster Unionists in defying parliament in resorting to force rather than accept Home Rule – this group were Europe's first fascists. It was these activities of F. E.'s which led to Casement's famous remark when, after he had been prosecuted by F. E. (who was then Attorney-General), he pointed out that if he had advocated treason so had the Attorney-General: 'The difference between us was that the Unionist champion chose a path he felt would lead to the woolsack – while I went the road I knew must lead to the dock.'

Casement's thrust must have struck home for Smith later was to say, 'Nothing has ever given me greater delight than the execution of Casement.'

This, then, was one of the men whom Griffith, Collins and the Irish delegation found themselves ranged against when they went over on the Treaty negotiations to conduct negotiations in the Autumn of 1921. Birkenhead had the reputation of being an honorary Orangeman whose prejudices had been welded in the hot forge of Liverpool Diehard Protestantism. But his great intellect was always subject to the impact of truth. One man on the Irish delegation fascinated Birkenhead – Michael Collins. Collins' lightning brain and his ability to get to the point astonished the Lord Chancellor whose training over thirty years had been directed towards achieving a similar mental agility. Here was this 'Paddy' who had never been to secondary school or university and whom Birkenhead had hitherto regarded as an appalling murderer, now revealing intellectual qualities that rivalled the greatest legal brain in England. Collins, clearly, was not in awe of Birkenhead, but appreciated that he was working with a first rate negotiator whose capacity for 'clear thinking, work and getting ahead' he deeply appreciated.

What is not generally remembered about the Treaty is that the right wing of the Conservative party regarded it as a monstrous betrayal of the empire – a surrender to the murderous 'Micks' of Sinn Féin. There were proposals at a Tory conference in Liverpool in 1921 that the government stop talking to 'the murder junta' and send in fifty thousand troops instead. By this time, however, Birkenhead had been converted by Collins to an idea of Irish freedom (almost as sensational a turn around since Paul slipped the saddle on the road to Damascus) and was determined to convince his party this was the correct solution. Three days before the Tory conference on 15 November, Birkenhead went up to Liverpool and there, using his unsurpassed gifts as an advocate, persuaded the leader of the diehards, Lord Salvidge, to agree to the terms of the Treaty. Salvidge swung the conference and Collins' proposals were accepted.

John Campbell points out in this biography that: 'Collins was brought to the point of signing by an assurance on the boundary question which turned out to be worthless.'

This is so, as Collins fully believed that what was left of the northern counties would be too small to remain viable: 'The South would save Tyrone, Fermanagh, part of Derry, Armagh and Down.'

But to imply, as the author does here, that Birkenhead, even unknowingly, was party to a deliberate deception of the Irish delegation seems unfair. After all, Birkenhead, once the Treaty was signed, continued to hope that the new Stormont parliament would sometime send representatives to Dublin instead of to Westminster and would urge the Ulstermen, in pursuance of this idea, to exercise the option offered by the Treaty and row in with the Irish State. This was a far cry from 'Galloper' Smith and the honorary Orangeman.

When the border was finally determined in favour of the Unionists in 1926 Birkenhead's party was out of office and it was a Labour government which presided over those iniquities which divide our country today.

Birkenhead and Collins demonstrated how an Englishman and an Irishman could work together in mutual respect despite differences of opinion. In temperament they resembled one another and physically they were not dissimilar – both handsome burly men of action.

Birkenhead belonged to a class, the Tory Democrats, who, descending from Disraeli, have continued into our day with politicians like Ian McLeod, Harold Macmillan and Edward Heath. It is from this group and not the Labour Party or their fractured offspring that this country will have the best chance of obtaining a solution which could set at rest the conflict of centuries.

15 January 1984

14. Frank Ryan – Republican

When someone was in the same class as your mother at college and you heard her talk about him from time to time, it seems almost as if you've grown up with him. I heard Frank Ryan's name mentioned so often at home that I felt I almost knew him. Later I wrote a play about him. He was a Celtic Studies student in Douglas Hyde's class at University College Dublin in 1925. It is a pleasure to record that Seán Cronin has written an excellent study of this excellent Irishman *Frank Ryan: The Search for the Republic*.

As a young man Ryan was very much a *Gaeilgeoir*. He protested in the name of Holy Ireland at the production of *The Plough and the Stars* in 1926 and was among the mob who broke up the play. When Frank Ryan was editor of *The Irish People* he wouldn't print any article by Frank O'Connor that he felt was derogatory of the Irish language, and when Peadar O'Donnell tried to introduce soccer notes to the paper Frank was scandalised and wouldn't have it. As he grew older, though, his nationalism broadened and he was a member of the Republican Congress group which broke with the IRA in 1935. When the Spanish war broke out Frank Ryan became the spokesman for the Republican Congress. He replied to Cardinal McRory who had encouraged General O'Duffy's Brigade to go to Spain and fight for Franco. 'May I assure your Eminence that as a Catholic I will take my religion from Rome but as an Irish Republican I will take my politics neither from Moscow or Maynooth.'

It was quite consistent with Ryan's character that having made a stand like this he would himself go to Spain to fight for the Republic along with 127 other Irish volunteers. Over there his bravery and his military skill were soon recognised and he finished up in a senior position in the army of the Republic. He was captured in 1938 and condemned to death by Franco.

Frank Ryan seems to have disliked the fact that the Irish had to fight with a British battalion. He couldn't get over the fact that the English officers, in what was meant to be a socialist army, still carried swagger sticks. He was outraged when the battalion commander, an ex-Black and Tan named Wilfrid McCartney, framed Terry Flanagan (ex-Dublin Brigade IRA) and Ryan had to travel up to the front to have Flanagan released: 'The bastard,' wrote Ryan afterwards referring to McCartney, 'wounded himself in the left arm on the day of his departure and got the London *Daily Worker* to say he was wounded by Fascist rifle fire near Madrid.'

Another member of the British battalion alongside whom Ryan was fighting was Captain George Nathan, who ironically had been on the other side as a Black and Tan in the Anglo-Irish War in 1921. Nathan, a dangerous psychopath, is now known to have murdered the Lord Mayor of Limerick, Michael O'Callaghan and the ex-Lord Mayor George Clancy on successive nights and then tried to have the murders blamed on the IRA.

Having been in jail for over a year, Frank Ryan was finally saved from execution by the intervention of the then Taoiseach, Eamon de Valera, who worked through Leo Kearney, the Irish ambassador in Madrid, to arrange Frank's 'escape' to Germany. Mr Cronin describes this deal with great skill and he has no doubt as to how it was brought off. An unlikely ally was the Duke of Tetuan who appealed to Franco on Ryan's behalf. 'Four centuries in Spain hasn't changed the O'Donnell,' Frank wrote, 'for all their queer sounding titles they're Irish at heart.' (The family name of the Dukes of Tetuan was

O'Donnell.)

By a strange stroke of fate, one of Frank's great friends when he was in Burgos jail was Father Mulrean, who had been chaplain to O'Duffy's Brigade, and of whom Frank said, 'He would rob His Holiness if he thought he could help me.

One of the great virtues of Mr Cronin's book is that he doesn't try to disguise Frank Ryan's role in Germany as others would have done. 'The IRA considered Frank Ryan as their representative there,' he tells us. It is quite clear that Ryan was prepared to use German help to assist in the struggle to get back the North. There has been an attempt to create antagonism between him and Seán Russell, the IRA chief-of-staff who died on the submarine going back to Ireland, but there is no evidence of this in the book. 'Seán and I were always good personal friends,' Frank wrote, 'and never more than during his last days. He died in my arms.'

Though his first attempt by submarine failed, Ryan nearly got back to Ireland two years later. It was arranged that a German spy and an engineer would fly over with him in a flying boat and land on an Irish lake. But the plane never did get to take off. Despite his exile from Ireland Frank Ryan always remained cheerful. 'If the *Murichu* doesn't come over for me I'll go home by parachute,' he wrote to his sister. 'I believe it's quite the fashion now.'

There's something extraordinarily attractive about the personality of this gay, handsome Irish Republican. 'I want to go back,' he wrote in 1944, 'so that I can play a part (and I really believe I could do a little) in unifying my friends to support Dev in his foreign policy, while reserving our rights to differ on other matters.'

Sadly, Frank Ryan died in Berlin in 1945 of natural causes, and was buried there until Niall Andrews arranged to have his body brought back in 1979.

There's been an effort by Irish Marxists to capture Frank Ryan for themselves. This book makes it quite clear that nothing could be further from the truth. 'Frank was no more a Communist than I was,' Tom Barry said. 'He was a patriotic Irish Republican with left-wing sympathies based I am sure on Liam Mellow's historic document smuggled out of Mountjoy Prison where I was a fellow prisoner in 1922.'

23 November 1980

15. Aubrey Beardsley

When, on the 16 March 1898, Aubrey Beardsley at the age of twenty-six lay dying he told the priest who had given him the last sacraments, 'By all that is holy, destroy my obscene drawings.'

Poor Beardsley had been persuaded by certain bigots that his superb drawings for the Lysistrata were indecent and on his deathbed this is what was torturing the unfortunate man. Today those drawings wouldn't raise an eyebrow, seen against the background of the man of genius who created them. But England then spurned her one great artist of the nineties, what Bernard Berenson called the 'art-hating Saxons' dismissed Beardsley as 'a butterfly who played at being serious', while in France and Germany he was the only English artist of his time who was taken seriously.

Aubrey Beardsley made his name at twenty-one with his drawings for Oscar Wilde's *Salomé*. They were extraordinary. Cruelty and lust boiled up from the page. Beardsley drew in black and white. But he could suggest more with a line than his contemporaries could do with a palette of paint. With a lightning dart of his pen he could make the white space of a page fill up like a voluminous skirt. He had been influenced by Japanese painting, but his work began an entirely new departure in art. Yet he was extremely humble. When Whistler, who had once criticised him, said, 'I was wrong, Aubrey, you are a great artist,' the poor lad burst into tears.

Sir Kenneth Clarke, the noted art critic has selected the best of Beardsley's drawings and put them together in a book with a long essay by himself on Beardsley. Sir Kenneth writes engagingly and he has selected a representative group of Beardsley drawings which are faultlessly reproduced in the book. Sir Kenneth tells us in his elegant style how Beardsley was dismissed by John Lane as a contributor from 'the Yellow Book', which had been sold largely on the strength of his work, because of the scandal surrounding his name which had been drummed up by the Mrs Grundys of his day. A fervent convert to Catholicism, Beardsley was courageous enough not to change his style but continued to publish his drawings in *The Savoy,* edited by Leonard Smithers. But the unfortunate artist had consumption and he died before he was thirty with the two people he loved most, his mother and his sister, by his bedside. Later Yeats would write a set of beautiful poems about Beardsley's sister Mabel.

Like the majority of art critics, Sir Kenneth lets himself go without much thought about his subject's influence on the art of his time. It is permissible to speculate that Beardsley influenced Munch, Kandinsky and Klee and perhaps Picasso, but it is frivolous nonsense to write as Sir Kenneth does 'that Beardsley had such an influence on Leon Bakst that one might say his drawings are the foundation of the whole Russian Ballet style from *Schehrazade* to *Aurora's Wedding*. In the first place the Russian Ballet style was not created by Bakst and in the second place a case could be made that the most typical of Diaghilev's ballets was *Petrouchka,* choreographed by Fokine and designed by Alexander Benois, who bears as much relation to Beardsley as Andy Warhol does to Titian.

The real difficulty with Beardsley's style is that it is too easy to imitate. Micheál Mac Liammoir, who was devoted to Beardsley's work, often complained to me that an artist who studied Beardsley too closely could end up by going down a tunnel from which it was impossible to emerge, and with no light at the end. The one major artist who was influenced by Beardsley, and who did not end in pastiche was Harry Clarke. He did, in the infinitely more difficult medium of stained glass, what Beardsley had done with his pen. But alas like Beardsley in his time, Clarke has not received recognition as a major artist of the twentieth century. Anyone interested in Clarke's work can have a look at the wonderful Geneva window in the Municipal Gallery.

There are some impertinences in this book which should be corrected. Kenneth Clarke is not a literary critic and has no right to call Oscar Wilde's *Salomé* 'rubbish'. Nor, even within the limitations of an essay, should he dismiss Leonard Smithers 'as a drunken Yorkshireman with no literary or artistic pretensions.' That drunken Yorkshireman is immortal as an art critic can never be because he gave to the world Oscar Wilde's *The Ballad of Reading Jail* when no publisher in England would touch it because of Wilde's imprisonment.

One should say, nevertheless, that Sir Kenneth writes less waffle than most art critics and in giving us this beautifully illustrated memoir has left art lovers in his debt.

29 April 1979

16. Field Marshal Lord Wavell

Archibald Wavell is unique among desert generals in that he was the only one of the famous men of those campaigns who was not Irish. Alexander (Tyrone), Auchinleck (Galway), Montgomery (Tyrone), Dorman-Smith (Cavan), Dick O'Connor (Killiney) were the best-known generals who came from here. But as well there were Creagh, Ritchie, Cunningham and Harding who were Irish. Wavell was thoroughbred English, a Wykehamist, who went to Sandhurst, soldiered in the Boer War, Flanders and finished up under Allenby in the Turkish campaign in the First World War. He was also, arguably, the greatest British general of the Second World War. Rommel said of him: 'Of all the British commanders I fought against he was the only one who showed a touch of genius.'

In an incredibly short period and with inferior equipment Wavell, with Dick O'Connor as his front-line general, broke the Italian army in Ethiopia and captured ten divisions before the summer of 1941. Later, as Supreme Commander South-East Asia, it was Wavell who made operative Orde Wingate's Chindits whose unorthodox concept of war broke the grip of the Japanese jungle armies in the Burma campaign. As Viceroy of India Wavell would almost certainly have minimised the desperate slaughter that took place after the British withdrawal in 1946 had he not been summarily dismissed by the Labour government.

Why, then, was such a man harried and hustled right through the war so that his abilities apart from his desert campaigns, were never really properly harnessed? Ronald Lewin in a new study, *The Chief*, has given us some of the answers. We learn that Wavell had one fatal flaw – he was rude to politicians. When Churchill wrote a furious letter after the withdrawal from Somaliland protesting at the small numbers of British casualties and demanding a court of inquiry, Wavell replied sarcastically: 'A big butcher's bill is not necessarily evidence of good tactics.'

Churchill, who had once been a professional soldier and fancied himself as a tactician, never forgot this put-down. From then on he was determined to get Wavell, and put him 'sitting under a pagoda tree' in some colonial post. In the end it wasn't Churchill who finished Wavell's career, but Attlee who sacked him in what must have been the rudest letter ever written to a great man by a prime minister.

Wavell had another disadvantage in the barracuda reefs of power into which he plunged in his various careers. He was a man of honour. As a young officer he was bitterly opposed to the Curragh Mutiny where British officers threatened to resign their commissions rather than march against the Orangemen in Ulster. 'The idea of these officers of the army going on strike is appalling,' he wrote. 'I think this is what it really amounts to over this business, and it is to my mind absolutely disastrous. What about the men. They can't resign whatever their opinions are.' It was typical of Wavell to think of the rankers' point of view. For his time he had advanced social ideas: 'No nation,' he once said, 'ought to pass its entrance examination to civilisation so long as it has an itch for war or possesses slums.' We can imagine the effect this sort of talk must have had on the imperialist war-hungry circles in which he moved.

Wavell had an astonishing gift which made him unique among his army colleagues – a phenomenal memory for poetry. In 1944 he published *Other Men's Flowers*, a poetry anthology in which every poem included was written down from memory. The anthology contained most the great poets of the English language and has sold more than any modern poetry book (228,000) and is still going like hot dogs. Even the title gives us a clue to Wavell's personality. He chose it from a charming phrase of Montaigne's 'I have made a bouquet of other men's flowers and none but the thread which binds them is my own.'

Mr Lewin in his biography maintains that Wavell did make mistakes as a general. He thinks he was wrong to dismiss the operations in Iraq and Syria as diversionary tactics. He is rather severe on Wavell's conduct of the war in South-East Asia. But Mr Lewin's criticism is written in the context of Wavell as a great general and is not designed to belittle him and could, therefore, provide a very useful corrective to John Connell's definitive biography.

9 November 1980

17. Survivors

In *Survivors*, the account by veterans of the Anglo-Irish war of their experiences, we find the authentic voice of Republican Ireland from the grass roots up, how they felt, how they acted, how they survived. It is a major contribution to Irish history and Uinseann Mac Eoin must be congratulated for having interviewed the contributors and laboriously turned their words into print.

All the versions here are from the anti-Treaty side, but no matter. Great men fought on both sides in the Civil War and it is for our generation to have the detachment to recognise this; eventually we may get down to analysing the causes for the conflict and make sure that Ireland will never again have to undergo such a tragedy.

What a variety of people talk through this book. Seán MacBride for instance, winner of the Nobel Prize for Peace and the Lenin Prize. Then there is Máire Comerford, among whose relations were three British army officers who won the Victoria Cross and whose mother was an Irish Ladies Tennis Champion as well as Lady Captain of Greystones Golf Club, in those days a very West British institution indeed. Nevertheless, when Máire asked her mother to act as 'aunt' for Michael Collins for three weeks to get the Castle murder gang off his shoulders, she did so willingly to help the cause.

It is hard to think of the gentle, refined Máire as we know her these days, setting out in January 1923, as she describes here, with Paddy McGrath (later executed by the Fianna Fáil government in 1941) to kidnap W. T. Cosgrave, the President of the Free State, and failing only because their car ran out of petrol.

Tomás Ó Maoileóin recalls meeting a British officer who was very friendly in the cells after 1916. This turned out to be Robert Barton, who later became a convert to the Sinn Féin cause because of the impact the conduct of the prisoners made upon him. Here is Ó Maoileóin's view of Richard Mulcahy, who was chief-of-staff of the IRA in 1921 and later went into opposition to Ó Maoileóin during the Civil War: 'Mulcahy I held in high esteem as a soldier at that time. He had been the power behind Thomas Ashe at Ashbourne in the battle against the peelers there on the Friday of Easter Week, when an inspector was killed and others wounded. I remember well the speech he made at one of the debates we had on what should be done when we got out: "Freedom will never come," said he, "without revolution, but I fear Irish people are too soft for that." "To have a real revolution, you must have bloody-minded fierce men, who do not care a scrap for death or bloodshed. A revolution is not a job for children, or for saints or scholars. In the course of revolution, any man, woman or child who is not with you is against you. Shoot them and be damned to them. *Do bhain sé sin geit asam,* as ye might say."' Ó Maoileóin adds: 'The trouble with the IRB was that it was allowed to exist too long.'

In the first weeks of the Civil War Ó Maoileóin was in jail when he was visited by Michael Collins, the commander-in-chief of the Free State army. Collins wanted to meet some of the IRA officers 'to put an end to this damned thing'. 'The three Toms will fix it,' said Collins, slapping his fist into his hand (he meant Tom Hales, Tom Barry and Tom Ó Maoileóin).

Tony Woods tells how during the occupation of the Four Courts there was close liaison between Liam Mellows and Seán MacMahon, quartermaster general of the Free State army. It seems clear now that Collins intended to get arms through to the north in order to allow the minority up there to defend themselves. Woods has a glorious story which illustrates the unreal atmosphere leading up to the Civil War. He was driving a commandeered Free State armoured car when he encountered a family friend, Colonel Frank Thornton, of the Free State army. Thornton shot at him without knowing who was in the armoured car and wounded him, but when he found out who it was he brought Tony straight to hospital and then in a panic rang a mutual friend: 'Look, I'm in a bit of a jam. I'm after shooting Tony Woods. The old lady (meaning Tony's mother) will have my life. Come over here and do something.'

Peadar O'Donnell's account, as one would expect from one of the great short story writers in the English language, is full of good stuff. As late as 1962 he and Dan Breen were at the gate of the American embassy to protest about Vietnam. When he started to read the document they were handing in, Dan said: 'Don't bother reading it to me. Sure any bloody letter you sign I'll sign.'

John Swift recalls that Alfie Byrne was the only MP who went to find out about him when he was interned in Wormwood Scrubs, and how good Alfie, though not a Republican, was about looking after prisoners.

What a fantastic experience to hear from someone still alive how John Butler Yeats, the poet's father, and famous painter in his own right, came up to her and said, referring to the purple stockings she was wearing: 'Oh, passionate legs. I bow to the maiden who has obtained millions of pounds' publicity for the Irish cause, without extending anything but her voice.'

The girl old Yeats was referring to was Norah Connolly O'Brien, James Connolly's daughter.

Tom Kelleher brings us up to date with his views on the northern situation today. 'I'm under the impression that if England leaves, the people there who oppose us now, will make no fight. I satisfied myself on that during the days I spent at Máire Drumm's funeral four years ago. They all told me that.'

The one flaw in this book is that the compiler has inserted oceans of footnotes which he uses at the end of each chapter to give his own version of history. He launches attacks on both Michael Collins and Arthur Griffith. Wading through a maze of statements he implies that the British allowed Collins a free run during the Black and Tan period, and avoided arresting him. Footnote 16 on page 132 has this: 'On another occasion during a break in conference, Collins indulged in some boasting. "You had £10,000 on my head," he said to Churchill; "the Boers had only £250 on yours." There was no particular price on Collins' head; the highest at that time was £1,000 on the head of Dan Breen.'

Here is how the incident actually happened, as told by Churchill, the only person who could have known about it besides Lord Birkenhead. 'Lord Birkenhead and I were left with Michael Collins meanwhile. He was in his most difficult mood, full of reproaches and defiances, and it was very easy for anyone to lose his temper. "You hunted me night and day," he exclaimed. "You put a price on my head." "Wait a minute," I said, "you're not the only one." And I took from my wall the framed copy of the reward offered for my recapture by the Boers. "At any rate it was a good price, £5,000." I said, "Look at me, £25 dead or alive. How would you like that." (Churchill's note: 'actually no such reward had been offered by the British Government, but I did not know this at the time').

It can be seen that the compiler has turned the story completely round to suit his point of view. He also accuses Arthur Griffith of having softening of the brain, and regrets that he was given any role in the national movement after 1916. It was Arthur Griffith who created the structure (abstention from Westminster and setting up of the Sinn Féin parliament and courts of law) which gave moral force to the military movement, and without which it could not have succeeded. He provided 'the water for the fish to swim in'. Dick Mulcahy once told me that Griffith definitely endorsed the military actions of the pre-truce IRA while Eamon de Valera was on his mission in America, and there is no evidence anywhere that he opposed physical force. As to softening of the brain, the surgeon who performed the autopsy after Griffith's death, diagnosed it as being caused by 'a subarachnoid haemorrhage'. We are told here it was 'more probably apoplexy'. Yet in spite of these minor flaws no future historian can write about the period 1916-23 without having recourse to this invaluable book.

5 October 1980

18. Confessions of an Art Addict

The American Jewish community has a special talent for helping artists and Peggy Guggenheim was born into this group. She grew up in great luxury in Manhattan and then married an American in Paris. It was the golden age then there of Joyce, Cocteau, Breton, Duchamp, Colette: Peggy Guggenheim met all these extraordinary people. Soon she began to buy the works of the artists. In the end she accumulated one of the great modern collections of the twentieth century. She opened a gallery 'Guggenheim Jeune' in London and later another 'Art of this Century' in New York where she was the first to sell Jackson Pollack, Mark Rothko, Robert Motherwell, David Hare. Now this rich and witty woman has published her memoirs in an entertaining book – *Out of this Century, Confessions of an Art Addict.*

Peggy Guggenheim certainly has a gift for slaying with words. Here's what she says about the woman who ran away with her first husband: 'Kay was a second rate novelist, but not quite bad enough in those days to make the large sums of money she did later.' Another person she accuses of being in love with her third husband and comments: 'I am furious when I think of all the men who have slept with me, while thinking of other men who have slept with me before.'

Peggy certainly had a husky track record, when it came to the opposite sex. After her first husband she went off with John Holmes, a Donegal man who had been decorated in the Great War and who was unable to write because his liver was hobnailed from drink as was discovered when he died at thirty-eight.

Next off she scooted with Douglas German, an English communist intellectual who tried to harness her great wealth to the party. After that was Max Ernst, the painter and when she left him she finished up with a young man who put Max Factor on his face, bleached his hair and wouldn't let her upstairs when he had his real friends in the house.

In between these were numerous other lovers. Marcel Duchamp, the painter was one, our own Samuel Beckett (Miss Gugggenheim alleges) was another. In her version Beckett took her home after a party and they stayed in bed for twelve days, drinking champagne in between. Oblomov was the name she gave him after the character in Joncharov's novel who didn't have the will to get out of bed. She remembers Beckett as, 'a tall lanky Irishman with enormous green eyes that never looked at you. He wore spectacles and always seemed to be far away resolving some intellectual problem.'

What fascinated her about Beckett was that she never knew at what hour of the day or night he might turn up. His unpredictability fascinated her which is a good tip for any young writer trying to get in with a rich American woman. Eventually she got over her infatuation, so much so that she tells us she said to Beckett one day. 'Oh dear, I'd forgot I was no longer in love with you.'

That's Peggy Guggenheim's version of the alleged affair. I'd like to hear Beckett's.

There are other inimitable word pictures in this book. When she met Jean Cocteau for dinner, Peggy noticed that he kept his eyes on the wall behind her, where he was looking at himself in the mirror, so fascinated that he couldn't take his eyes off himself.

Peggy Guggenheim gave Joyce a shillelagh for his fifty-sixth birthday. She noticed, when she went to Joyce's apartment how close a family they were. This was an unusual circumstance in the Bohemian atmosphere of the Latin quarter. On the table at the party was a plaster model of Dublin with green ribbon running through it to represent Joyce's beloved Liffey. Afterwards Joyce did a jig and sang a song with Giorgio, his son, who was a professional baritone. He sent Peggy a Limerick to thank her for her present.

> Go caccanny with the cognac and of the wine fight shy
> Keep a watch upon the hourglass but leave the beaker dry
> Guest friendliness to callers is your surest thief of time
> They're so much at Holms when with you, they can't dream of Guggenheim.

Despite her unstable relationships with men, Peggy Guggenheim brought up her two children well. Her son Sindbad grew up to be an intelligent together young man, a cricket fanatic, who edited an exciting magazine in the forties in Paris which had the distinction of being one of the first to publish the works of the young Brendan Behan.

Peggy Guggenheim seems to have been a vulnerable woman who never gave up trying and in the process achieved a certain distinction. 'The incredible thing is,' she wrote at the end of her life, 'that I never believe in failure and no one can convince me that I cannot move mountains or stop the tide until I've proved to myself that I can't.'

30 March 1980

19. Pádraic Pearse – His Letters

In the preface of this collection of letters, edited by Séamas Ó Buachalla, the eminent historian and provost of Trinity College, F. S. L. Lyons says: 'These letters are bound to change the popular view of Pearse. . . they will not diminish his reputation; rather will they place it on a firmer and more credible basis.' Dr Lyons thinks that many readers will be surprised by: 'the rigorous exclusion of the poet and dreamer from a scene dominated by the able organiser and devoted headmaster.' He continues: 'These are the letters of a man who knew exactly where he was going and what he was doing, a characteristic in itself sufficient to set him apart from the great majority of his Irish contemporaries.'

What is remarkable about this collection is the breadth of Pearse's acquaintances. We find him writing to Lady Gregory, congratulating her on her play *Kincora* at the Abbey and asking her to work with him 'as allies' for Ireland. Pearse was also a great admirer of Yeats and was delighted when the poet offered to put on one of Pearse's plays, *An Rí,* at the Abbey to raise money for St Enda's. 'Was it not very good of Yeats to do this for us?' he writes to a friend in March 1913. In the same year, he can still praise John Redmond, reminding him of his courage, 'when you stood on Parnell's right hand when the baying of savaging hounds was loud in his ears.'

If there is one quality that distinguishes the letters, it is courtesy and tolerance of other people's opinions. If only, for instance, Pearse's view of Irish Ireland had been adopted by the Department of Education and the

Gaeilgeoirs in the twenties and thirties, how much better position the Irish language would be in today. 'What I mean by an Irish school,' Pearse wrote, 'is a school that takes Ireland for granted. You need not praise the Irish language – simply speak it: you need not denounce English games – play Irish ones: you need not ignore foreign history and foreign literatures – deal with them from the Irish point of view.'

Pearse's whole life centred around his school, St Enda's. To create an institution where he could put his educational ideas into practice was an immense task at that time. We can take Provost Lyons' word that 'Pearse was a brilliant and forward-looking schoolmaster,' but the Catholic Church did not want laymen in charge of schools at that time. Dr Dwyer, Bishop of Limerick, had stated: 'No layman has the right to teach.'

Nevertheless, Pearse got going and eventually he succeeded in purchasing a beautiful mansion at the foot of the Dublin mountains to house his school. Here, the boys elected their own captains and house leaders and took a ballot to decide what games they would play – a mini-democracy. Pearse's thoughts on the function of teaching could be put over the door of any school in Ireland, or any school elsewhere for that matter. 'The true teacher will recognise in each of his pupils an individual human soul, distinct and different from every other human soul that is nearest and most akin to it, craving, indeed, comradeship and sympathy and pity, needing also, it may be, discipline and guidance and a restraining hand, but imperiously demanding to be allowed to live its own life, to be allowed to bring itself to its own perfection: because for every soul there is a perfection meant for it alone and which it alone is capable of attaining.'

It was indirectly through St Enda's that Pearse got in touch with the extreme wing of the Irish Republican Brotherhood. Desperately in need of funds, he went to America in 1914. There he found that the only people who were really prepared to help him in his educational project were IRB leaders like John Devoy and John McGarrity. It is from these men that he first got the idea of an armed revolution as a solution to the Irish problem. From his letters written before 1915, it is quite clear that he believed his work for Ireland would be at St Enda's and that he looked forward to enlarging the school when the war would be over.

There are all sorts of interesting details to be gleaned from the letters. For instance, we learn that one of the governors of St Enda's was Shane Leslie who was a first cousin of Winston Churchill (though the editor doesn't mention this relationship). In a letter written in 1904, Pearse suggests forming a Union for Irish Journalists, anticipating the National Union of Journalists. While he was on ship for New York, he remembered that his mother hadn't been to the pantomime and sent her money to buy tickets for herself and his sister. He cautions an over-ardent Gael against wearing trews at a Feis instead of a kilt, since even though the trews might be more authenticly Irish, he ran the risk 'of leading the spectators to imagine that you have forgotten to don your trousers and had sallied forth in your drawers.'

Mr Ó Buachalla has done a splendid job in collecting these letters and putting them together for publication. There is one little touch of fuzziness, though, that should not be allowed to go unchallenged. He calls the 1937 Constitution 'a Republican one'. It was not, any more than the one it replaced – the 1922 Free State Constitution.

3 August 1980

of his years as a schoolmaster at a Quaker school in Swanage, Dorset, and of how he fell in love with one of his girl pupils there. The various characters who inhabit the school spring to life before our eyes. You can smell the disinfectant in the classroom, the leather overcoats and riding whips in the hall, hear the constant chatter of the schoolchildren, see them on their outings against an enchanting pastoral landscape of Dorset. The detail is meticulous as in this description of an autumn ride with his pupils across the Dorset lanes: 'Here the children would dismount, stuffing the pockets of their riding breeches or jodhpurs with chestnuts. When these were full they would force chestnuts down into their woollen stockings so that their calves and shins bulged with strange eruptions as they rode home.' There is a description of a strange thatched theatre in a wood with three women doing mime to Mussorgsky's music and singing Elizabethan lyrics behind closed curtains. The horrors of the First World War had not, it seems, killed the spirit of William Morris.

Against such a background Monk Gibbon describes the effect of his pupil on him. There are no gropings, passionate embraces, couplings here. He only kisses his pupil twice (the second time when she is in her mid-twenties). On each occasion it was no more than a feather brush. This is a description of love generated by the electricity which two personalities send out, and not by sexual contact. There is a precedent in the poetry of the troubadours for this form of love as a vehicle for art. Poets like Bernard De Ventador influenced by Moorish poetry sang exactly this way of their ladies in the courtly schools of Provence and Sicily. This tradition reached its highest form in Dante's love for Beatrice and Petrarch's love for Laura. Now in our time Monk Gibbon has [illegible]created the tradition in an Anglo-Irish context. I think [illegible]ould regard George Moore as his examplar in [illegible]raphical prose. Yet Moore's work oozes [illegible]hile Gibbon has made an art form out of restraint.

There are no rules in art. If a writer can put himself under a microscope and let us see him squirm he fulfils a function. But it must be a microscope to reveal all and not a rose-tinted window to disguise nature. Monk Gibbon gives himself to us exactly as he is and in shedding the protection which most men use to live lives of quiet desperation he accepts the vulnerable stance of the artist. He is the last in a great tradition of writers who burst upon the Irish scene in that extraordinary decade before the First World War, Yeats, Lady Gregory, George Moore, AE, Synge, Gogarty, Colum. One would hope that a plaque to honour him would be placed on his father's rectory in Dundrum so that an important Irish writer could have recognition in his own lifetime.

22 November 1981

21. Samuel Beckett

Jack McGowran, the Dublin actor, introduced me to Samuel Beckett in a Paris café in 1964. I had just written a book in which there was a chapter about Beckett's part in a Dublin libel action. I mentioned this to Beckett (the book was about to be published). He murmured in reference to the case, 'It should never have happened.'

He seemed to me without malice. On his long handsome face, there was a mask of sorrow rather than venom. A man who, feeling the pressures of the artist, had reacted with compassion rather than savagery. As the night wore on, the graven lines on his face loosened and he listened with intense merriment to Jack McGowran's very funny Irish stories. In between the chat, we were questioned carefully about our sports careers. (McGowran had been an Irish highjump champion.) When Beckett said goodbye, his very tall figure and El Greco face reminded me of a Spanish Grandee. He showed great concern about our taxis.

One of the values of Deirdre Bair's biography is that it brings out aspects of Beckett's character which could not be guessed at by those who only read his books or watch his plays.

Beckett has become the apostle of despair in the eyes of readers throughout the world, the artist who had denied the existence of order in the universe. Yet in the nineteenth century sense of the word, he has always retained a sense of duty. He fought for the Maquis (the French Resistance) against the German occupation of France. He served with the Irish Red Cross with exceptional devotion in 1946. He has a high sense of family responsibility. Both his mother and his brother had lingering deaths. Beckett was constantly at their bedsides to bring whatever comfort he could to them.

These actions, if we examine them, are however not inconsistent with Beckett's rejection of an ordered universe. He believes that it is possible to find a way that will represent chaos in artistic form. But he has set out to find a new form independent of the concept of an established order. He has peeled away skin after skin in an attempt to find the 'it' which is himself.

This process can be painful. Deirdre Bair takes us through different periods of Beckett's life, when he went through his personal Gethsemane. He seems to have been a depressive possessing the steel will of the artist which enables him to emerge enriched from the darkness with an enlarged vision of life, and to depict the horrors he has gone through.

When a critic pressed Beckett for his views on form in art, he replied, 'I was in hospital once. There was a man in another ward dying of throat cancer. In the silence I could hear his screams continually. That's the only kind of form my work has.' Instead of the whine with which Sartre has greeted the same predicament, Beckett responds with a shrill laugh. The bad eyesight, the rotten teeth, the repeated plagues of boils which troubled him throughout his lifetime are reminiscent of the physical tortures which Joyce endured in pursuit of his art.

Like Joyce, Beckett's rejection by the public was, at one time, total. His first novel, *Murphy,* was rejected by forty publishers. *Waiting for Godot* was only produced, after many rejections, in a little underground theatre in Paris in 1951. The text of the play was published in New York and in its first few years only sold a few copies. Today over a million copies have been sold.

Beckett had a characteristic, though, which Joyce lacked – an inherited toughness of frame which came from two centuries of Anglo-Irish professional stock. Swift had this physical endurance, so had Yeats. In the frightful years of deprivation which are described in this book, Beckett was fortunate that his prowess as an athlete had left him with an exceptionally good body which could withstand illness when the germs moved in to attack. He was a superb cricketer at Trinity and a champion boxer and rugby player at Portora Royal School in Enniskillen. He could indeed have qualified for one of Yeats' 'swift indifferent men'. He and the poet don't seem to have met very often. But Beckett has a high regard for Yeats as I discovered at a performance of *The Countess Cathleen* in Paris when Beckett quoted admiringly from the great lines at the end:

> The years like great oxen
> tread the world. . .
> And I am broken by their
> passing feet.

Deirdre Bair's book is marred by inaccuracies. She attributes a story to me that I could never have told her for the simple reason that the first time I knew of the events described in it was when I read it in this book. It is quite incorrect, indeed outrageous, to state that 'Jack McGowran turned to pills and liquor', and that 'he spent most of his working hours in a zombie-like state.' McGowran, a close friend of mine, was a teetotaller for the last years of his life, and when I would meet him, I never noticed him in a trance.

Nevertheless with any faults it may have, by reason of her access to unpublished letters, especially those written to Thomas McGreevy, and to others, material which has not so far become available, Deirdre Bair has produced an intriguing study of a man of genius.

22 October 1978

22. The Politics of James Joyce

At the beginning of this book the author, Dominic Manganiello, quotes a statement of James Joyce to his wife Nora in order to prove that Joyce was politically orientated: 'I hope the day may come when I shall be able to give you the fame of being beside me when I have entered into my kingdom.' Now this is no more a political aspiration than the advertisement on the side of a bus. Joyce is referring, of course, to some time in the future when he will have had recognition as a artist. His political stance is best indicated by a statement to George Borach in 1918: 'As an artist I attach no importance to political conformity.'

A written reply he made to the *Geneva Journal* in 1916 underlines this sentiment: 'I am restricted to making personal pronouncements by means of the scenes and characters of my poor art.'

But as the book progresses, Dr Manganiello, while he does not succeed in convincing us that Joyce was a political animal, does reveal a surprising interest in politics on Joyce's part. Joyce was, for instance, an early admirer of Griffith's Sinn Féin and wrote prophetically in 1906 that: 'Either Sinn Féin or British Imperialism will conquer the present Ireland.'

Joyce admired Griffith because he was 'holding out some secular liberty to the people against the church' and he noted with pleasure, when he came back to Ireland before the war to negotiate the publication of *Dubliners* that: 'Griffith received me very kindly', having printed a savage letter of Joyce, about censorship in the face of possible libel threats.

When he lived in Trieste Joyce frequently wrote articles and gave lectures on Irish history in which some of his political attitudes emerge. For instance, in an article in the *Piccolo della Sera* in 1907 he pointed out that while Fenianism was still a separatist doctrine, the movement no longer approved of dynamite: 'From many points of view this last phase of Fenianism is perhaps the most formidable. Certainly its influence has once more remodelled the character of the Irish people. The most fervid enemy of Irish Catholicism is the head of English Catholicism, the Duke of Norfolk.'

Perhaps the most consciously political act that Joyce ever undertook was his challenging of the British Consulate in Zurich during the war over an alleged swindle that Joyce believed took place when he presented some plays in English there. He hadn't been particularly impressed by England's attitude at the start of the war: 'England goes to fight for liberty in Europe but junkerdom in Ireland' was his comment. He sensed the backlash in the attitude of the English diplomats to him in Zurich. After a bitter battle he finally got some sort of satisfaction from Sir Horace Rumbold, the consul. Terence MacSwiney was dying on hunger-strike at the time when Joyce wrote this verse which certainly would have delighted Griffith had he read it:

Of spinach and gammon
Bull's full to the crupper,
White lice and black famine
Are the Mayor of Cork's supper
But the pride of old Ireland
Must be damnably humbled
If a Joyce is found cleaning
The boots of a Rumbold.

By far the most fascinating parts of this book are the chapters in which Dr Manganiello has traced how Joyce's obsessive interest in the politics of the Free State (derived from reading Irish newspapers), surfaces in *Finnegans Wake*. Dr Manganiello makes a very good case indeed for identifying Mr de Valera with Shaun the hero of that section of *Finnegans Wake* known as *Tales Told of Shem and Shaun*. He relates the mysterious quarrel between Shem and Shaun to the conflict over Document No 2 in the Treaty debates. He has picked out a number of references to 'dim delty Deva', 'dev do espart', 'devourced', 'Da Valorem' which help make his point that Shaun and the author of 'Decumens numbered too' are one and the same person.

Also from the jargon of *Finnegans Wake* Dr Manganiello has unearthed material which may give us an insight into Joyce's secret feeling about post-1922 Ireland. For instance, one of the characters argues that freedom in the south is preferable to fealty to Britain in loyal Ulster: 'You are up-in-Leal Ulster – and I'm-free-down in Easia, this is much better.' Dublin is described as 'a phantom city. . . bowed and sould. . . for a price partitional of twenty six and six.'

Despite the claims of this able book, however, the fact remains that Joyce placed his art above country and religion and refused to involve himself in anything that might hinder its progress. Cunning was his weapon and he modelled himself on Homer's devious hero 'the only man in Hellas who opposed the war, and because he thought up the strategem of the wooden horse.'

18 January 1981

23. An Unhusbanded Life

Her brother was Viceroy of Ireland in 1920 with half a dozen mistresses and a famous military record. She motored through Ireland with Maud Gonne at the height of the Black and Tan terror investigating British atrocities, and publicising them abroad. Charlotte Despard was seventy-five but she had been a freedom fighter all her life. She was one of the first to campaign for women's rights, and had been a founder member of the Women's Freedom League. Living in a working-class area of London, she had created a miniature welfare state for the poor, walking the streets in habit and sandals, inviting the destitute back for food, clothing and a bed, to the large building she owned and lived in.

Charlotte Despard was one of the heroic band who fought at the turn of the century to undermine the principle of all-male government which underlay the imperial system. She had been in jail on numerous occasions, and had had her property seized for refusing to pay tax in protest against unjust laws. She was an heiress in her own right, and one of the reasons it was suggested that her brother, General 'Jonny' French was reluctant to take action against her was that he owed her so much money, borrowed to pay for his mistresses. Charlotte was a Catholic theosophist and a militant socialist. But there is nothing of the crank in her. She simply had a larger idea of freedom than most people of her time. 'The end of war or famine,' she said once, 'they're all impossible dreams, but the dream must be dreamed until it takes a spiritual hold.' She achieved many of her 'impossible dreams' simply by getting on with the job. 'I've always believed in discontent,' she told a reporter, 'not grumbling, which is usually selfish and individual, but a disinclination to sit down idly knowing things are wrong.'

After the Civil War (in which Charlotte took the anti-Treaty side) she bought a house in Clonskeagh, 'Roebuck', where she and Maud Gonne lived for some time. Republicans on the run, people in trouble, released prisoners, all found shelter there. Genteel ladies organised a jam factory, which was intended to make the Roebuck establishment pay its way.

Now Andro Linklater (Eric Linklater's son) has written a splendid biography of this remarkable woman. He traces her career from the time she was a rich young society girl till she fell down the stairs and died at the age of ninety-five in a house in Whitehead, near Belfast. Mr Linklater is very good indeed on Charlotte Despard's Irish period, and gives a admirable summing up of the circumstances which led to the Anglo-Irish War in 1919. He makes one or two small mistakes. Mick Price, the IRA chief-of-staff was not, as Mr Linklater says, 'bitterly anti-communist' but in fact led the socialist breakaway in the IRA in the early thirties. Mr Linklater also comments on the title Madam, which many of the lady revolutionaries assumed in the twenties. 'This title conveyed both popular esteem and a popular conception that the people who had it were not Irish.' This is nonsense. There were many ladies who were called Madam, and who were of impeccable Irish descent, such as Madam O'Rahilly. I, myself, had an aunt who was a Madam, and who made jam up in Roebuck House. If anything, the title had French Revolution overtones.

Mr Linklater maintains that Charlotte Despard's involvement with Ireland was not because of her Roscommon blood, but because of her concern with freedom, and that the national aspect of the struggle was of little significance to her. This could be true. Having founded the Irish Workers' College, with a grant given to Roddy Connolly (later, ironically, a supporter of

Cruise O'Brien in the Labour Party), Charlotte skipped it to Belfast where she felt there was more need for freedom fighting than in the South. At that time Belfast was a really frightening place, where Catholics were regular victims of pogroms from police and para-militaries, who operated with the tacit permission of the Stormont government. In a letter, Charlotte described what she had witnessed in Ballymacarrett, near St Matthew's Church. Sixty years later, these words have a familiar ring. 'Having visited many panic-stricken families and inspected their houses riddled with bullet holes, I stood talking with some of the women. Everything was quiet. The people stood about in little groups before their doors. The children were playing. Suddenly there was a pistol shot fired from an armoured car. Panic followed and the children ran into any open door. I was drawn by trembling women into the cottage of an ex-soldier, a man who had fought in Belgium and Gallipoli. Volley after volley from rifles and machine guns swept the street and this went on with brief intervals for an hour and a half.'

Charlotte stormed into the offices of the Minister of Home Affairs, Sir Dawson Bates, but he just commented that 'the B Specials were a fine body of men' and rudely turned his back on her. Nothing daunted, she sought an interview with the Prime Minister, Sir James Craig, and addressed him in what can only be described as prophetic words: 'Go on as you are doing,' she told him, 'give your legalised gunmen carte blanche to shoot, maim and insult their fellow townsmen and to destroy their homes: keep thousands of men idle and as sure as day succeeds night retribution in an awful form will come to you.'

Charlotte Despard lived on until September, 1939. She was ninety-five when she died, and active till the end. She had never allowed her mind to settle into a mould. 'Human nature is dynamic,' she insisted, 'it changes, it moves, great forces act upon it. . . Old moulds are broken and new moulds are ready for the expanding life.'

She asked to be buried in the Republican Plot in Glasnevin and her body was brought down from the North for the funeral there.

Sadly, her great love of freedom and for equality between the sexes has not been realised in the Irish Republic. No woman judge, one token Minister of State, no woman head of a State body, is a poor record for a revolution which has fought to achieve freedom for all.* On the other hand, the country to which she devoted the first part of her fight for freedom for women, now has a woman Prime Minister.

* This was written in July 1980. Today there are two women ministers and one woman High Court judge.

24. Todd Andrews

Growing up in Dublin in the forties you heard round the family table names like Dick Brown, 'Pussy' Leyden, Tommy McLoughlin, Fred Boland, Charlie Bewley, John Hearne, Joe Walsh and Todd Andrews. You realised that they had a great deal to do with the running of the country though they were not politicans. Later you learned that they were public servants who came from both sides of the fence in the Civil War and had been prepared to sink their differences to get this country on the move. But the sort of people they were or what contribution they made was information not easily come by. Public servants are by profession anonymous and do not have books written about them.

Now one such public servant, Todd Andrews has come along with one of the most riveting books I've read for years, *Man of No Property*.

Andrews came from a Dublin family who had sufficient money to put him through University College Dublin. But he went there with a stigma. He had fought on the anti-Treaty side in the Civil War. University College Dublin was fiercely Cumann na nGael. The other side was looked on as little more than gougers with nothing better to do than snatch poppies from loyalists on 11 November. Todd Andrews' crowd at College, on the other hand, disapproved of top hats and morning clothes, horse racing, golf, tennis, white flannels and even people who got married with a red carpet. They were mostly from Christian Brother backgrounds and resented what they regarded as the condescending attitude of those who came from private boarding schools and accepted wholeheartedly the Free State regime. How Todd Andrews and his anti-Treaty contemporaries came to recognise the merit of those on the opposite side and worked in tandem with them in the public service is recorded here, in the prose of a born writer.

The Free State had their Shannon scheme and their Electricity Supply Board. The Fianna Fáil crowd had their bogs and their Bord na Móna. In the middle were the public servants who had to see that political grievances were submerged when it came to getting the job done. Todd Andrews had a dream as a little boy when he used to play in Shaw's Wood in Bushy Park to transform the Bog of Allen into the Forest of Allen. 'A country whose bogs support only grouse and snipe was to me a backward country'.

When Fianna Fáil came to power Andrews got his chance to turn the bogs into a source of energy and power. He decided to find out what the Germans and Russians were doing about their peat. Extended visits to both countries by groups of Irish officials and engineers led to the setting up here of the Turf Board which would ensure that we could endure four years of neutrality during the Second World War without having the economy collapse for lack of fuel and power. The author depicts the enthusiasm and ferocious work schedules of these pioneer days in a way that makes it sound like an adventure story. They believed in the hunch rather than on the safe solution and had as a maxim 'he gives twice who gives quickly' to encourage quick decisions as against bureaucratic delay.

Todd Andrews has a gift for sketching character and the personalities of his colleagues crackle to life under his pen. There are plenty of exhilarating anecdotes, like the time Maria Duce picketed the Bord na Móna offices in Pembroke Street in protest at the visit of a Russian delegation, and Andrews had to pretend to the communists that it was a welcoming party.

In 1952 Todd Andrews left Bord na Móna for Córas Iompair Éireann. He was then fifty-four years of age. He regards his failure to revive Córas Iompair Éireann and bring the bus workers along with him as 'the biggest disappointment of his public service career'. He puts the blame on 'weakness in trade union management organisation' and thinks unofficial strikes 'supported by the near-mystical respect of the picket line should be made illegal'. He retired from Córas Iompair Éireann and became Chairman of Radio Telefís Éireann in 1963. Here one begins to glimpse the tendency of the man of action to indulge in the comfortable protection of red tape. He speaks, for instance, disapprovingly of the 'irresponsible mentality of the creative people'. In Radio Telefís Éireann his remedy for this seems to have been to approve the appointment of an engineer as Director-General, though how this profession endows people with an ability to decide matters concerned with entertainment, news, sport and drama has never been properly explained.

In fact as we read the later chapters in this book, those devoted to his experiences in Córas Iompair Éireann and Radio Telefís Éireann, we begin to suspect that Todd Andrews himself became a victim of the system. Now he writes more as a bureaucrat than as a free spirit who ranged across the Irish bogs with such adventure in the first chapters. It's in the nature of the bureaucrat that he is reluctant to accept criticism from the public. Was it, one wonders, the trade unions in Córas Iompair Éireann that were at fault and the 'creative people' in Radio Telefís Éireann? Was it not a rigid management structure that failed to communicate to the work force and sealed itself off in complacent contemplation of its own excellence which has given rise to galloping doses of Parkinson's Law in both organisations?

The mistake of discontinuing the Harcourt Street line when foresight would have indicated that with the projected increase in car traffic it could have become an invaluable transport artery, one feels would have been unacceptable to the man one reads about in the early part of this book.

One of the features of the book is the author's gift for

sketching a vivid pen picture. Frank Aiken is described as 'an engineer manqué' who in another age would have been an alchemist. Todd Andrews believes that Cearbhall Ó Dalaigh had the characteristics of a sixteenth century humanist and who, if he had lived in that time, would have been 'a renaissance man befitting the company of More and Erasmus'.

Others do not come off so well. Gerard Sweetman reminds him of 'Flashman in *Tom Brown's Schooldays,* arrogant and a bully'. Charlie Bewley, the Irish minister in Berlin, is dismissed as 'a very grand person who was said to know every baroness in Berlin and every countess in Rome by the diminutive form of their Christian names.'

W. T. Cosgrave also gets a hard time. When de Valera asked Todd Andrews why W. T. remained aloof, Todd Andrews pointed out that de Valera in a letter to Joe McGarrity had 'referred to Cosgrave as a "ninny" and in his deep heart's core Cosgrave knew that the description was appropriate but could not forgive the perception it prompted: it was like catching a man with his trousers down.' This is manifestly unfair. Cosgrave was a man with elements of greatness who pulled the State together after a disastrous Civil War when it could have collapsed entirely. Subsequently when out of office he did his country another good turn when he refused to countenance authoritarian groups in his party and once again restored politics to the democratic process. He was a man of personal courage, having been condemned to death (but pardoned) as vice-commandant of the South Dublin Union in 1916, a fact often forgotten. Such are the scars of the Civil War that an author of Todd Andrews' calibre should have written about him in this way. The author here quotes de Valera as saying that the Constitution was entirely the work of John Hearne, the legal advisor of the Department of External Affairs, and that Dev's own contribution amounted to 'only dotting the i's and crossing the t's'. This is not exactly true, as I know from John Hearne himself. He told me that as he and Dev left the Government Buildings on the night they had finally finished drafting the Constitution he said to the Taoiseach: 'How does it feel to be walking out into a Republic?' A look of extreme concern passed over Dev's face and he immediately asked Hearne to go back into the office again where, with the help of the Protestant lawyer he had advising him, they re-drafted the section dealing with Ireland's relationship with Great Britain.

Todd Andrews has the virtue of being completely frank in his views. He believes that Lenin was one of the great men of history who 'was moved to loathing of the exploitation of the many by the few. For himself he sought neither glory nor riches.' He writes a good deal in this book of his sympathy for socialism and 'particularly the communist movement'. On Northern Ireland his stand is firm. 'Orangemen are not English or hyphenated Scots-Irish. I believe our common nationality forges a common bond of mutual understanding and appreciation. England continues over the centuries to be the source of our political ideas. Given a British withdrawal with benevolent good will I believe an accommodation could be reached with our Northern fellow countrymen.'

There is a Rousseau-like freshness in this book, the determination of the author to present himself and his times, warts and all, which make it a valuable contribution to the history of the new state.

12 September 1982

25. Sir Oswald Mosley

I met Sir Oswald Mosley in the fifties. I was naturally interested to talk to someone whom the Labour cabinet minister, Richard Crossman, had described in the *New Statesman* as follows: 'He was capable of becoming either Conservative or Labour Prime Minister and reveal himself as the outstanding politician of his generation. Mosley was spurned by Whitehall, Fleet Steet and every party simply and solely because he was right.'

Of course I had read about Mosley's fascist past, his massed Blackshirt meetings at Earlscourt before the war, the anti-Jewish activities associated with his organisation, the British Union of Fascists, and their association with Hitler and Mussolini. . . Having an ingrained horror of anti-Semitism I questioned him about the accusations that had been levelled at his organisation. 'We had Kid Berg, the Jewish East End world welter-weight champion as one of my bodyguards,' he replied with a disarming smile. 'It was only later, because of what was happening elsewhere with Fascism, that Jews refused to join the movement.'

This argument didn't seem quite to add up and I subsequently found it was a distortion of the facts. Mosley seemed less anxious to defend his pre-war position in regard to the corporate state. Now he wanted Union in Europe – Germany, France and England joined together against the Bolshevik menace. His favourite book was Goethe's *Faust*. Later he sent me the most recent English translation to read. There was no doubt that in his cultural outlook he was drenched in European literature and philosophy. The last time I saw him was in his little jewel of a palace outside Paris called, of all things, the *Temple du Gloire*. There, while his beautiful wife, Diana, listened attentively (I find it difficult to comprehend that, according to this book, she kept photographs of Hitler and Goebels on her mantlepiece while her country was at war with Germany) Mosley talked about his plans for a new political system and his loss of faith in the parliamentary process: 'What is the point of a parliamentary system that pays a Prime Minister £10,000 a year to run the country and a leader of the opposition £2,000 to stop him.'

Mosley's interest in Ireland had been benevolent. As a returned war hero and a member of the Tory party, he had mercilessly exposed Black and Tan atrocities here in 1921. He had a gift of making one want to accept what he was saying even if one felt that the logic was askew. After a while you began to grasp that his thinking was a synthesis of Nietzsche and Bernard Shaw: 'We must deliberately accelerate evolution; it is no longer a matter of volition but of necessity.' All right in theory. But dangerous stuff when applied to the sawdust ring of politics. I remembered how off beam Shaw had been when it came to political judgment. It seemed to me that Sir Oswald's flair was for literature and philosophy rather than politics.

Now Nicholas Mosley, Sir Oswald's son, has written a brilliant book about the second half of his father's career and his own reaction to the events that Oswald Mosley was involved in. As a fourteen-year-old in 1939 Nicholas had witnessed the extraordinary meeting in Earlscourt when his father was in a black shirt and his hand held high in the Fascist salute had addressed many thousands of the faithful just as Hitler did at Nuremburg, ending with an astonishing peroration: 'And now, lit by the flame of such high inspiration, this movement rises from the very soul of England to give all, to dare all, that England may, that England will live in greatness and in glory.'

Shortly afterwards, the war began and Nicholas Mosley found himself a pupil at Eton while his father was in jail. Mosley had been imprisoned for being in alleged sympathy with the Nazis and a threat to the King's realm. Nicholas stood firmly by his father at this time as is shown by his letters from school: 'Of course, all the boys believe every word the papers say and worship that fool, Mr Churchill. I found it does not pay to try and tell them how wrong they are. The sensible ones, including me, are just waiting for Eton to be bombed so we can all go home.'

Having left Eton, Nicholas went to Balliol to sit for an exam but found the place 'stiff with Jews'. Later he joined the army and fought in the Italian campaign as a captain in the London Irish Rifles, winning an MC for gallantry. From the battlefront he wrote back to his father long, discursive letters containing references to Descartes, Schopenhauer, D. H. Lawrence, James Stephens (one of Oswald Mosley's favourite authors) and, of course, politics.

When he returned to civilian life after the war, Nicholas still looked on his father as a great man who had been done down by lesser ones. The theme of this extraordinary book is how Nicholas slowly came to see his father in a different light. The first time he had doubts was when he began to question why the Mosleyites, before the war, had held the majority of their meetings in a predominantly Jewish area of east London. If the British Union of Fascists were not anti-Semitic, why should they want to stir up unnecessary trouble. Then, in the fifties, his father seemed to be getting excessively shirty about the black population in Britain. He would insist on going down to Notting Hill Gate with his supporters and advocating, from a public platform, that coloured people be deported to a new national home. This, naturally, led to a conflict between the new Union movement and the blacks. One day in 1959 Nicholas stood at the back of a meeting where his father spoke as a British Union candidate for North Kensington: 'There was Dad on top of a van again and bellowing – so much older now with his grey hair and grey suit. I expected that he, at least, would be putting over the aspect of his case that was reasonable, but, instead, I still find it difficult to believe this – but other witnesses have confirmed it, there he was, roaring on about such things as blackmen being able to live on tins of cat food and teenage girls being kept by gangs of blacks in attics.'

Blind with fury, Nicholas confronted his father the following day and told him he no longer believed in his policies. Sir Oswald's reply was, 'I will never speak to you again.' However, the father did make it up with his son. But the relationship would be on a different basis. Nicholas was no longer an acolyte. He had seen behind his hero's mask.

The way Nicholas Mosley has written this book, a mixture of biography and autobiography, makes it read like a novel. He demonstrates in a way that a novel never could how a man of talent, even genius, can be perverted by the system into a negative force. Mosley's blueprint for social reform, when he was a Labour minister in 1928, formed the basis for much of Labour's post-war policy in Britain. The trouble was, when his solution was rejected, Mosley simply couldn't wait (as Churchill did) till the course of events would prove him right. He was in too much of a hurry. Perhaps this was the aristocrat in him. He was aware of the futility of his own class when it came to solving the problems of his country but he was unwilling to wait for a solution to be found through the popular vote – the democratic process. Once he had passed the point of no return he, like all men of authoritarian outlook, became mesmerised by his own importance, refused to listen to criticism, and sowed the seeds of his own destruction. To have chronicled this transformation must have been heart-rending for the author. But he has honoured his father by not bending the facts and introducing us to a form of biography which could be looked on as a work of art.

11 December 1983

26. Cyril Connolly

Few people have influenced a generation as Cyril Connolly did. His two seminal works, *The Unquiet Grave* and *Enemies of Promise*, supplied every up-and-coming literary acolyte with a new working vocabulary and a large repertory of erudite quotations in French and Latin. Connolly even popularised a word which became a catchcry of the post-war era, 'angst'. Most people were understandably scared out of their wits of another conflagration during the Cold War, and to suffer from 'angst' or insatiable worry was considered essential to the literary stance of the late forties and early fifties.

Then, there was Cyril Connolly's magazine, *Horizon*. He was one of the great literary editors in history. Like Ezra Pound, he had an infallible nose for the new. *Horizon* bulged with brilliance and vigour. Connolly was a Francophile and knew what was going on in Paris, as well as being wired in to most of the new movements in the arts elsewhere. He could judge the contributions that were sent to him against the background of European trends instead of, as most of his contemporaries did, in the context of an insular Anglo-Saxon outlook. It was he who, for instance, gave Patrick Kavanagh an international fillip when he accepted *The Great Hunger* for *Horizon*.

Now, David Pryce-Jones has published *Journal with a Memoir*. This book has not so far had a good press. I found it fascinating, the private thoughts of an international man of letters, what one would expect from a Gide, Mauriac or Sartre. What has put a lot of English critics off, I think, is Connolly's contempt for the country he grew up in: 'One cannot really love London,' he wrote having returned there once. 'It is unsatisfactory in every way, a foggy dead-alive city like a dying empty antheap,' or 'I boil with Anglo-phobia – you've no idea how degenerated, physically, the English are,' or, 'Back in England: feel nothing but an intense disgust at its stupidity. Fatuous newspapers. . . the wireless with its children's corner, reports of tennis matches, lectures on the composition of the cricket team, on the searchlight tattoo, absurd music. Miss Ivy St Helier beginning, "Don't be afraid, I'm not highbrow." Nor she is.'

What comes through in these diaries is that Cyril Connolly, old Etonian and Balliol scholar was irrevocably caught in the Celtic labyrinth. His Irish connections were the Vernons of Clontarf Castle (an old Norman family) and the Connollys of Castletown. At school he had adopted the personality of Tim Connolly, 'Irish rebel, a backhanded tribute to the events of 1916' and later, at Oxford, he tried to explain to Harold Acton (the original of Anthony Blanche in *Brideshead Revisited*) and Raymond Mortimer why he seemed to lack the urge to get on that was common amongst his contemporaries: 'I said it was not the scholar in me that was incurious, but the Celt. I happened to have a good intellect and a classical education, but underneath there lay the Celtic dreaminess, incuriosity, and tendency to brood.'

Brood he might but he had an insatiable, frenzied appetite to learn about the world outside which took him on mammoth journeys to Italy, Spain and France before he was twenty-five. Dressed in khaki shorts and a college blazer, an old Etonian tie, and a Basque beret on top of his monkey-like head, he was an oddity. But he knew this and like the Anglo-Irish eccentrics from which he descended, he cultivated his originality and made himself into a personality which the languid decadents who formed the majority of his contemporaries of Oxford were not. It is interesting that Joyce, notoriously reluctant to see English literary folk, liked Connolly. When they did meet the two talked about the lanes around Clontarf,

Irish cricketing families and the beauty of the River Dodder. Connolly obviously wasn't the only oddity in the company. Later he wrote, 'Only the Irish are impressed by exile. It knocks the Celtic twilight out of them. Joyce, Moore, (Yeats a spiritual exile whining after Colonus and Byzantium)'.

Connolly's other Irish friends were Billy Clonmore, the jovial earl with the chiselled features of George IV, who became a great character in the Dublin bars of the fifties, and Piers Synnott who wore two buttonholes and one of whose last compositions before he died three months ago (which he sent me) was a brilliant parody of 'God Save the Queen' celebrating the visit of the bold Mr Fagan to Her Majesty's bedchamber. The writer Connolly seems to have felt closer to was Gerald Brenan, another Anglo-Irishman related to Lord Edward Fitzgerald, who was a devotee, like Connolly, of Arthur Whaley's *Lady Murasaki*.

When Connolly died in November 1974, a whip-around had to be organised for his widow. He left not a cent, but instead, substantial debts. A failure? Quite the contrary. With a relatively small output he had made his mark on his generation in a way that men of enormous output but no genius have not. He always doubted his position but he had an odd moment of confidence when he said to David Pryce-Jones in 1961: 'I had nothing but my talent – they had colleges, cliques, pensions, the party line. Born in Coventry I'd have died in coventry if they had their way. Yet, because I had something to say, I am read.'

21 August 1983

Bibliography

1. *Selected Plays* by Lennox Robinson. Gerrards Cross: Colin Smythe.
2. *Façades* by John Pearson. London: Macmillan.
3. *Prodigal Father: The Life of John Butler Yeats* by William Murphy. Cornell University Press.
4. *In the Wake of Diaghilev.* Autobiography by Richard Buckle. London: Collins.
5. *Patrick Kavanagh – Sacred Keeper.* A Biography by Peter Kavanagh. Dublin: Goldsmith Press.
6. *The Letters of Evelyn Waugh.* Edited by Mark Amory. London: Weidenfeld and Nicholson.
7. *Desire and Other Stories* by James Stephens. Selected and introduced by Augustine Martin. Dublin: Poolbeg Press.
8. *Annotations to Finnegans Wake* by Roland McHugh. Baltimore: Johns Hopkins University Press.
9. *Harold Nicolson. A Biography* by James Lees-Milne. London: Chatto and Windus.
10. *The Journals of Lady Gregory* edited by Daniel J. Murphy. Gerrards Cross: Colin Smythe.
11. *John Masefield – A Life* by Constance Babington Smith. Oxford University Press.
12. *The Great Hunger. Ireland 1845-9* by Cecil Woodham-Smith. London: Hamish Hamilton.
13. *F. E. Smith, Lord Birkenhead* by John Campbell. London: Jonathan Cape.
14. *Frank Ryan, The Search for the Republic* by Sean Cronin. Dublin: Repsol Publishing.
15. *The Best of Aubrey Beardsley* by Sir Kenneth Clarke. London: John Murray.
16. *The Chief. Field Marshal Lord Wavell,* by Ronald Lewin. London: Hutchinson.

17. *Survivors.* Edited by Uinseann Mac Eoin. Dublin: Argenta Publications.

18. *Out of this Century, Confessions of an Art Addict* by Peggy Guggenheim. London: André Deutsch.

19. *The Letters of P. H. Pearse* edited by Séamas Ó Buachalla. Gerrards Cross: Colin Smythe.

20. *The Pupil* by Monk Gibbon. Dublin: Wolfhound Press.

21. *Samuel Beckett* by Deirdre Bair. London: Jonathan Cape.

22. *Joyce's Politics* by Dominic Manganiello. London: Routledge and Kegan Paul.

23. *An Unhusbanded Life* by Andro Linklater. London: Hutchinson.

24. *Man of No Property* by C. S. Andrews. Cork: The Mercier Press.

25. *Beyond the Pale: Sir Oswald Mosley* by Nicholas Mosley. London: Secker and Warburg.

26. *Cyril Connolly: Journal and Memoir* by David Pryce-Jones. London: Collins.

MORE MERCIER BESTSELLERS

Communications and Community in Ireland

Edited by **Brian Farrell**

To mark World Communications Year 1983 Radio Telefís Éireann broadcast a series of ten Thomas Davis Lectures dealing with the role of communication in the evolution of the modern community in Ireland.

These lectures now published in book form afford the reader the opportunity of seeing highlighted some of the major phases, incidents and personalities in the history of the media in Ireland. The series also links the Irish experience to comparable developments elsewhere and uses individual local cases to illustrate some general themes of modern mass communication studies.

Men Withering

Francis MacManus

There is little need to introduce the writing of Francis MacManus. For many years his books have charmed all who have gently relaxed into his world of Irish rural life.

For over three decades, he wrote in English and Irish for publishers on both sides of the Atlantic. He has written essays, reviews, short stories, biographies, travel books, history and, above all, novels. The biographies range from the life of that Italian master of the sensual, Giovanni Boccaccio, to a life of the most austere of Irish saints, Columban of Bobbio. The novels also range over a wide area of human life – Ireland in the eighteenth century, New Mexico in the twentieth. *Men Withering* is centred around the life of the famous Irish poet, Donnacha Ruadh Mac Conmara. Francis MacManus was on the staff of Radio Éireann since 1947 until his untimely death in 1965.

'That's How It Was'

Kevin Danaher

Irish folk tradition is a wonderful mixture of fact and fancy. Many people believe that our forefathers were so simple and credulous that they believed everything they heard. This is not true and although there were people who would swallow any tall story just as there are many people today who believe every word in television advertisements the average person long ago knew the difference between the fact and fiction that abounded in folk tradition.

Stories believed to be true, especially tales of past happenings were always certified by the saying 'That's how it was', indicating that the *seanchaí* believed it and you had better believe it too, at least within his hearing!

With Kevin Danaher we travel the roads with the farmers and drovers on the way to the fairs and we meet the *spailpíns*, tramps, tinkers and the travelling musicians and listen to them swap greetings and gossip. We travel the roads our forefathers walked, we rest under the trees that shaded them and we pass the walls that heard their songs and their laughter.